Expecting Multiples:

The MOST Comprehensive Guide to High-risk Twin & All Triplet, Quadruplet or More Pregnancies

2nd Edition

Expecting Multiples:

The MOST Comprehensive Guide to High-risk Twin & All Triplet, Quadruplet or More Pregnancies
2nd Edition

Edited by:
Diane K. Wipfler, OTR/L
MOST Chairman & Associate Medical Director
Maureen A. Doolan Boyle
MOST Executive Director

Contributing Editors:

Kelly Ross, MD

John T. Boyle, MD

John P. Elliott, MD

Victor R. Klein, MD

Wendy Noriega, RN, BSN

Tina Lomaka, RN, BSN

Patti Tessler, RN, FNP

Lauretta Shokler

Pam Chay, RN, IBCLC

Laurie LaMonde, PhD

Marsha Pike

Acknowledgements

This book could not have been written without the contributions of many people.

We would like to thank all the MOST families who contributed quotes and photos as well as their experiences about having a multiple birth family.

Thanks also to all the professionals, MOST volunteers and MOST staff members who contributed to this book by sharing their experiences, expertise and knowledge.

Published 2013 by MOST (Mothers of Supertwins)

Revised 2013

PO Box 306

East Islip, NY, USA

Revision written and compiled by

Diane K. Wipfler OTR/L and Maureen A. Doolan Boyle

ISBN 978-0-578-11046-2

Printed in USA

MOST dedicates this book to all the future parents of triplets, quadruplets, quintuplets, sextuplets and more.

Preface

"Congratulations on your pregnancy! I know how terrifying this can be because I felt the same way. I think I may have cried for weeks, but as time went on, things got better. Now I look at my triplets and cannot imagine life without them. It certainly helps to have someone to talk with, so try to contact anyone you know who has triplets or more. You can also benefit from chatting with MOST families. Sometimes I felt like the only person who was going through what I did, but I quickly learned I was not alone. My pregnancy went well. I carried to 34 weeks, and the babies were in the NICU for 2 weeks. Everyone is different, but if you have a doctor who is proactive and with whom you feel comfortable, that makes a world of difference."

C ongratulations on the exciting news about the impending arrival of 2, 3, 4, 5, or more new family members! Expecting multiples can be scary but also exciting as well. As the mother in the quote above states, you have found a wonderful resource in MOST (Mothers of Supertwins). MOST, founded in 1987, is a national support network of families who are expecting or parenting twins, triplets, quadruplets or more.

Even though MOST supports all multiples, the materials in this book focus primarily on higher-order multiple pregnancies and high-risk twin pregnancies. Higher-order multiples are defined as triplets, quadruplets or more.

Being in touch with families who have been down the same road makes all of the difference during a high-risk pregnancy such as a higher-order multiple gestation. MOST believes each parent is entitled to and obligated to become a health care advocate for his or her children starting from the time of conception. To accomplish this, parents must be educated health care consumers, and the information in this book is a great place to start. Through education, MOST strives to empower families with the information they need to make informed decisions about pregnancy, child development, and ultimately the children's education.

I am the mother of triplets who were born in 1987 and to two singletons (one before and one after our triplets). My singleton pregnancies were not considered high-risk pregnancies, and during both I delivered around my due date. My triplet pregnancy was at the opposite end of the spectrum. This high-risk pregnancy included medications and technologies to help prolong my pregnancy, antepartum (before delivery) hospitalization and a premature delivery. My husband, Jack, and I are so very fortunate to have healthy and active children today, but we appreciate the challenges families as ours face getting to this point. Families who are expecting higher-order multiples or high-risk twins should know that pro-active prenatal care significantly increases the chances of having very healthy babies. Your goal is to have big babies born close to term, and our mission is to help you achieve that.

Many parents of multiples find that life is a little different from the lives of their family, friends, and neighbors. MOST families experience joy and challenges, pleasure and pain, frustration and simplicity: much more intensified than most families can imagine. The little pleasures in life hold new meaning with multiples: weeks or months of bedrest during pregnancy, blurred memories of sleepless nights with newborns, potty training a group during the toddler years, managing so many new routines during the elementary school years, and finding the courage to teach 2, 3, 4, 5, or more teenagers to drive as they near adulthood.

Come meet the many wonderful families here at MOST who are managing the blessings and trials of raising their multiples through the MOST website, MOST Family Support Forums, and our many social media outlets. If at any time we can help you or your family, please let us know. MOST has a vast array of resources and information on every stage of parenting multiples ready and waiting.

At MOST, we are very aware that there are many types of families, including single parents by choice, same-sex partners, adoptive parents, and many others. Throughout the book we use terms like partner, mother and father, but our use of these terms does not imply disrespect or lack of support for other situations. MOST offers support and resources for all types of families and uses these terms for simplicity.

Maureen Doolan Boyle, MOST Executive Director

Contents

INTRODUCTION..15

   About MOST (Mothers of Supertwins)..15

     What is MOST?...15

     What is MOST's Mission? 15

     What Type of Support Does MOST Offer Families?...................16

     How is MOST Funded?...17

     How Do I Contact MOST?..17

CHAPTER 1: BASIC FACTS ABOUT MULTIPLES 19

   Incidence and Definitions of Multiple Births......................................21

   Diagnosing a Multiple Birth Pregnancy...23

   The Role of Fertility Treatments in Multiple Births...........................24

   Average Gestation and Outcomes 26

   Fraternal versus Identical: About Multiple Birth Zygosity 29

   Fetal Reductions..31

   References...36

   Resources 36

     Incidence of Multiples...36

     Identical Twin and Twin-to-Twin Transfusion Syndrome...........37

     Pregnancy Reduction/ Selective Reduction.................................37

     Fertility Treatment..38

CHAPTER 2: PROACTIVE PREGNANCIES 39

   Choosing Your Doctors 41

     High-Risk Pregnancy Analogies..43

     How to Find a Maternal-Fetal Medicine Specialist.....................43

     Not All Maternal-Fetal Medicine Specialists are Alike 44

     Suggested Interview Questions for both Obstetricians and MFMS....44

     Advocating for Your Babies...47

Choosing a Hospital for Delivery 48

Types of Neonatal Intensive Care Units (NICU) *49*

What to Look for in a Level III NICU *50*

How to Find a Good Level III Neonatal Center or NICU *56*

Relocating for Care 56

Special Note for Dads and Significant Others 58

Keeping Track of Concerns 59

Care of Teeth and Gums 60

Prenatal Classes 61

Preparing for the NICU 62

References 65

Resources 65

Maternal-Fetal Medicine Specialists *65*

NICU Preparation *65*

CHAPTER 3: PRENATAL CARE **67**

A Perinatologist's Perspective on Managing Higher-Order Multiple Pregnancies

by John Elliott, MD 68

Weight Gain and Nutrition: Goals and Expectations 78

Why Nutrition is So Important *78*

What is the Optimal Weight Gain? *79*

How To Enhance Optimal Weight Gain *81*

How To Avoid or Decrease Constipation *81*

Planning Your Calorie Intake *83*

References 88

Resources 89

Pregnancy Weight Gain *89*

Medications during Pregnancy *89*

CHAPTER 4: POSSIBLE CHALLENGES AND TREATMENTS DURING PREGNANCY ..**91**

Morning Sickness and Hyperemesis 92

Tips for Managing Hyperemesis *93*

Treating Hyperemesis *94*

Infections 94

Urinary Tract Infections (UTI) 94

Yeast Infections 94

Vaginal Bacterial Infections 95

Fifth Disease 96

Anemia 97

Carpal Tunnel Syndrome 98

Round Ligament Stretching 99

Twin-to-Twin Transfusion Syndrome 99

Definitions Related to TTTS 100

Symptoms of TTTS 100

Treatment of TTTS 101

Gestational Diabetes 102

Symptoms of Gestational Diabetes 102

Skin Changes During Pregnancy 103

HELLP Syndrome 105

Poor Fetal Growth (Fetal Growth Restriction) 106

PUPPP 106

Vaginal Bleeding 107

Preterm Premature Rupture of Membranes (PPROM) 109

Losses during Pregnancy 110

Effects of Early Partial Loss 113

Effects of Complete Loss 113

Effects of Late Partial Loss 114

References 116

Resources 116

Hyperemesis 116

Anemia 116

Carpal Tunnel Syndrome 117

Twin-to-Twin Transfusion Syndrome 117

Preeclampsia 117

Loss during Pregnancy 117

CHAPTER 5: TESTS AND TREATMENTS...**119**

Ultrasounds and Biophysical Profiles (BPP).................................120

Ultrasounds...*120*

Frequency of Ultrasound Tests *120*

Ultrasound Types *122*

Reasons for Conducting an Ultrasound................................*124*

Amniocentesis and Chorionic Villus Sampling.........................124

Amniocentesis...*124*

Chorionic Villus Sampling...*125*

Corticosteroids...126

Cerclage...126

Pessary..127

CHAPTER 6: PRETERM LABOR AND BEDREST...**129**

Preterm Labor: What It Is 130

Signs and Symptoms of Preterm Labor 131

Preterm Labor: What You Can Do 132

Steps to Help Prevent Preterm Labor *132*

Steps to Take When Experiencing Symptoms of Preterm Labor *133*

Self-Palpation for Contractions *134*

Diagnosing and Treating Preterm Labor...................................135

Fetal Fibronectin *135*

Tocolytics *137*

Bedrest..142

Bedrest Activity Level and Bedrest Activity Checklist.........*142*

Tips for Managing Bedrest..*145*

Fetal Movement Monitoring..*149*

Long-Term Hospitalization Prior to Delivery 151

Items You May Wish to Have With You at the Hospital.........*151*

Tips to Prepare Children for Mother's Hospitalization.........*152*

Resources 155

11

Preterm Labor..*155*

Tocolytic Medication *155*

Bedrest *155*

CHAPTER 7: PREPARING YOURSELF, FAMILY AND HOME, ...**157**

Preparing Yourself..158

Arranging Help *158*

Naming the Babies *159*

Preparing to Breastfeed...*159*

Journaling...*162*

Questions about Personal Concerns and Care *162*

Preparing Your Family 168

How Fathers and Significant Others Can Prepare...............................*169*

Helping Older Siblings Prepare *169*

Including Grandparents and Other Family Members...........................*171*

Preparing Your Home 171

Baby Showers...*172*

Layette and Useful Equipment and Supplies.....................................176

Clothing *176*

Baby Equipment...*176*

Furniture..*177*

Diapering Supplies *178*

Bath Supplies *179*

Feeding Supplies for Breastfeeding or Pumping *180*

Feeding Supplies for Bottle Feeding..*181*

Medical Equipment..*182*

Other Supplies..*183*

Items NOT to Buy...*184*

Resources 186

Finding Help or Childcare..*186*

Product Safety and Medical Release Forms *186*

Feeding Charts, Color Coding and Getting Organized.........................*187*

Car Seats..*187*

CHAPTER 8: DELIVERY **189**

Vaginal Delivery of Higher-Order Multiples....................................190

C-Sections & Combined Deliveries..191

Scheduled C-Section versus Emergency C-Section...........................*192*

Delayed Interval Deliveries 194

Postpartum Recovery..195

Leaving the Hospital: You and Your Babies 196

'Full-Term' or Late Preterm Babies 198

References...199

CHAPTER 9: PRACTICAL CONSIDERATIONS **201**

Personal and Marital Stress...202

Coping with the Stress of Parenting Multiples.................................*204*

Insurance and Financial Concerns 205

Postpartum Depression..207

Do I Have PPD? *208*

Why Should I Seek Treatment?...*209*

What Treatments are Available? *209*

Online Safety and Security for Your Family 210

Resources 211

Marital Stress and Multiples...*211*

Postpartum Depression..*211*

Insurance and Medical Bills *212*

Personal Information and the Media *212*

CHAPTER 10: AN ENDING AND A NEW BEGINNING...............................**213**

Helpful MOST Resources..214

INDEX...**219**

Introduction

About MOST (Mothers of Supertwins)

What is MOST?

MOST (Mothers of Supertwins), a community of families, volunteers and professionals founded in 1987, is the leading national nonprofit provider of support, education and research on higher-order multiple births.

What is MOST's Mission?

MOST's mission is to advocate for quality prenatal care, promote healthy deliveries, and supply information to all multiple birth families in order to support successful parenting through every phase of their children's development.

Many women contact MOST for preconceptual counseling or very early in their pregnancy and stay in touch throughout the "Bedrest Blues" and possible antepartum (before delivery) hospitalization. One of our main goals is to help make your pregnancy easier and decrease anxiety through education from professionals and support from mothers who have also experienced a high-risk twin or a higher-order multiple pregnancy, birth, and parenting.

MOST also conducts medical and psychosocial research projects to better serve our families by identifying specific needs and trends in care and outcome.

Through these national projects we can help educate the medical and ancillary support professionals about the unique needs of higher multiple birth families. MOST asks families of multiples to complete a MOST Medical Birth survey, which covers conception, pregnancy, delivery and the first few months with your multiples. Throughout this book this survey will be referenced as it provides important information for families such as yours. Also in this book, researchers, doctors, and other health and educational professionals can find data from the MOST Medical Birth survey to develop tools and information for families.

As in the general population, our families often have a variety of challenges/situations unassociated with parenting multiples. Having multiples adds another level of complexity to these issues. We are here as a conduit for all of our families during all stages of pregnancy and parenting to address both multiple birth related issues and those that are not.

What Type of Support Does MOST Offer Families?

MOST provides support in many ways. Some of the most frequently utilized support includes one-to-one contact from one of our MOST Mentors (trained MOST

volunteers) or the office staff. MOST also offers several online forums and educational materials for parents related to multiples. A more extensive list of MOST support and informational resources is available in the last chapter of this book.

How is MOST Funded?

MOST operates on a combination of grants and donations. As a non-profit organization, MOST exists through the generous support of families and professionals. Visit the donation page www.MOSTonline.org/donation.htm for information on ways to support MOST. For every $1 donated to MOST we are able to provide over $3 in services thanks, in great part, to the generous work of our volunteers. Almost all of our volunteers are the parents of multiples like you.

How Do I Contact MOST?

Mothers of Supertwins (MOST)
P.O. Box 306
East Islip, NY, 11730
(631) 859-1110
info@mostonline.org
www.MOSTonline.org

Where else can I find MOST?

Look for MOST on the web. Currently, MOST is on Facebook, Twitter, LinkedIn, and Flickr. We also have a blog at www.MOSTonline.org/wordpress.

Important Notice: This book was written to provide you with information and support while you are pregnant with 2, 3, 4, or more babies. This book is **NOT** intended to provide individual medical advice and should **NOT** be used in lieu of consulting a qualified medical professional.

Chapter 1: Basic Facts about Multiples

Congratulations on your pregnancy! MOST is here to help you every step of the way: through all your decisions (and there will be many), through all the milestones, and through all the ups and downs of your pregnancy and parenting. Families begin in many different ways. All of our families are unique. Here are just two family stories.

Laura and Bill married and wanted to have a baby. Just one baby. They figured after a while that they needed help to conceive. After seeing many doctors and going through many tests, the doctor helped Laura become pregnant. They were going to have the child they had dreamed of. When Laura went for her first visit with her doctors after her pregnancy was confirmed she had quite a surprise. Three babies! What started as a simple, normal pregnancy quickly became a high-risk pregnancy. Now what?

After having two children Heather wanted one more child. She quickly became pregnant. When she went to her obstetrician she was shocked to find out she was pregnant with triplets! She noticed she seemed larger but had thought it was because this was her third pregnancy. Now what?

Like these families during their pregnancy, you are not alone. **MOST is here to help you...every step of the way.** With the information in this book and other resources as well as support from MOST and our families, you can find the best solutions to the challenges you will face. No matter your story or how your pregnancy came to be, you may have the following questions.

- Now what?
- How can I do this?
- Will the babies be okay?
- Will my wife be okay?
- Do we need a specialist?
- Is he/she in our town?
- Will we need to relocate?
- How will we afford this?
- Will my insurance cover all that my babies will need?
- How will we pay for diapers?
- Do we need to move or get a new car?
- How will we pay for college?

This book will help answer some of those questions and others as well as help you make decisions so you can be the best parent you can. For many decisions there is no right or wrong and you may later feel you made some mistakes, but with information and support from MOST, you can make the most loving decisions possible and be content that you did.

Incidence and Definitions of Multiple Births

We have included this information so you can better understand what a multiple birth is, how often they occur, how they are diagnosed and the use of fertility treatments in multiple births. The following list gives the type of multiple births by the number of babies involved in the pregnancy:

21

1 baby = singleton	6 babies = sextuplets
2 babies = twins	7 babies = septuplets
3 babies = triplets	8 babies = octuplets
4 babies = quadruplets	9 babies = nonuplets
5 babies = quintuplets	10 babies = decaplets

The Centers for Disease Control (CDC) publishes birth statistics for the US annually. Usually the report covers data from two to three years earlier, so in 2012 the statistics for 2009 were published. According the Centers for Disease Control's National Vital Statistics Report "Births: Final Data for 2009":

- 33.2 twin births occur per every 1,000 total live births

- 1.535 triplet or more births occur per every 1,000 total live births

In 2009, 143,625 live multiple birth babies were born in the United States:

- 137,217 twins

- 5,905 triplets

- 355 quadruplets

- 80 quintuplets and above (1)

Due to medical advances in fertility therapy, the chance of having a multiple birth has increased in the past since the 1980s; however, that trend is slowly reversing for births of triplets or more. The rate of triplet births peaked in 2002 and has slowly been declining or holding steady since. Known factors that increase the odds of having a multiple birth (twins and above) include:

- Being an "older" mother (particularly women over age 35)

- Being a taller than average mother

- Having a previous birth of fraternal twins/multiples

- Having a history of fraternal multiples on the mother's side of the family

- Using fertility medications and/or assisted reproductive technology [See MOST's Supertwins 101 FAQ #4 (www.MOSTonline.org/faq4.htm)

for more information on the use of fertility treatments and the risks of conceiving triplets or more.]

MOST encourages prospective parents who are undergoing fertility treatment to thoroughly discuss the potential benefits and risks of any proposed treatment course with their health care practitioners. We are happy to offer such individuals information about parenting higher-order multiples and to refer expectant parents to high-quality sources of information for pregnancy and parenting. [See the MOST Recommendations on the Responsible Use of Fertility Treatments (PDF): www.MOSTonline.org/FertilityTreatmentsandMultiples.pdf.]

Diagnosing a Multiple Birth Pregnancy

"Telling my husband was more fun than telling our parents. When I had my first ultrasound it was triplets. Bruce was golfing and I called him on the course and told him. He was thrilled. Two weeks later when I went back and they found the fourth baby – he was in his car...I think he pulled over when I told him! My next ultrasound...he definitely went with me!"

For couples undergoing fertility treatments multiple gestations are more common and a higher than expected blood pregnancy test level (the hCG level) early in pregnancy can suggest a multiple gestation. However, the only way to confidently diagnose more than one baby is an ultrasound exam. Usually transvaginal ultrasound (when a wand is placed into the vagina), as early as 6 weeks gestation, is used to diagnose a multiple birth pregnancy. Sometimes fetuses may be missed in higher-order pregnancy but that is rare. For those pregnant with a spontaneous pregnancy, often the first sign of multiples is a uterus that measures larger than expected. For example, the uterus of a pregnant mother measures the size of a 15-week gestation despite only being 10 weeks along.

The Role of Fertility Treatments in Multiple Births

"I am new to MOST and 9 weeks pregnant with triplets. We transferred 3 blastocysts on a 5 day transfer and were told we had up to an 11% chance of having triplets. I wonder what happened!"

"I was 30 years old and after several years of trying to conceive, much discussion and much research we decided that we did not want to take a chance of having multiples. If needed, we would have several IVF transfers rather than take a chance of having multiples by transferring more than one embryo. I was young and we thought that we had some time. With the help of our Reproductive Endocrinologist, we decided to have a single embryo transfer (SET). You cannot imagine our shock when we learned that we were carrying triplets! How could that be? Our single embryo had split, twice, and we now had an identical triplet pregnancy."

Photo by Claudia Akers Photography

According to the 2009 CDC report titled "2009 Assisted Reproductive Technology Success Rates: National Summary and Fertility Clinic Reports," 146,244 assisted reproductive technology (ART) cycles that year resulted in 37,780 pregnancies and 45,870 live births. Of those, 29% were twin pregnancies and 3% were triplet, quadruplet or more pregnancies.[2] The CDC defines ART as including all fertility treatments in which both eggs and sperm are handled. That means any procedure involving surgically removing eggs from a woman's ovaries, combining them with sperm in the laboratory, and returning them to the woman's body. Also donating eggs to another woman is an assisted reproductive technology. Sometimes, but not always accurately, ART is referred to as "test tube babies." ART does not include treatments in which only sperm are handled (i.e., intrauterine or artificial insemination: also called IUI) nor does it refer to procedures in which a woman takes medications only to stimulate egg production (ovulation inducing medicines or ovulatory stimulating medications) without the intention of having eggs retrieved.

The MOST Medical Birth survey data shows that approximately 85% of triplets are the result of some type of fertility treatments and around 15% are conceived spontaneously without the use of medications or technology. The percentage of spontaneous conceptions in the MOST survey decreases for quadruplets to approximately 4%, and <1% for quintuplets or higher. While not common, certainly not all triplets, quadruplets, or even quintuplets are the result of fertility treatments.

Due to recent improvements in many ART procedures and recommendations for the increased use of techniques like single-embryo transfers (SET) by organizations such as the Society for Assisted Reproductive Technology, the percentage of respondents to the MOST Medical Birth survey indicating their higher-order multiples were conceived as a result of one or more ART procedures has declined dramatically.

Since 2003, more respondents to the MOST Medical Birth survey indicated conceiving their higher-order multiples following the use of ovulatory stimulating medications alone rather than the use of one or more ART procedures. While statistics are available on how ART procedures have affected the number of multiple births, statistics on how ovulation induction, through the use of medications alone or with insemination, affect the number of multiple births are not collected in the US at this time.

How you conceived your multiples does not matter to MOST. We support all families of multiples whether you have undergone fertility treatment to become pregnant or not. We understand that some couples have spent months and sometimes years coping with challenges and losses beyond your control. If you did not use any medications or procedures to become pregnant, then you may be quite shocked that you are having more than one child! However you became pregnant, the ultimate goal is a healthy pregnancy. With that said, you need to know that a higher-order multiples pregnancy is a high-risk pregnancy.

In addition, after the babies are born, families face the awesome challenges and fantastic gift of parenting 2, 3, 4, 5, or more children all at the same time. We encourage friends and family members to offer positive support for your choices once you are expecting multiples. These pregnancies are not usual but your desire to become a parent is nothing but normal and needs to be supported. Positive support is important and can be very beneficial to both you and your children.

Average Gestation and Outcomes

A full term baby is born between 39 to 41 weeks of gestation. Rarely does any multiple birth pregnancy last a full 40 weeks. It is actually strongly recommended that triplet pregnancies not go past 37 weeks and quadruplets not past 35 for reasons as complications increase at that gestation. These reasons will be discussed more later in the book. More than 58 percent of twins, more than 94 percent of triplets, and virtually all quadruplets and higher multiples are born preterm. (3) Preterm or premature refers to delivery before 37 weeks gestation.

Important Notice: The numbers listed here represent the average week most expectant mothers delivered; however, these numbers are not the GOAL! It's also important to keep in mind that even if you reach the optimum goals, your babies will still be considered premature and not full-term infants.

The CDC reports the average gestational week reached is:

- 38.7 weeks for singleton pregnancies
- 35.3 weeks for twin pregnancies
- 31.9 weeks for triplet pregnancies
- 29.5 weeks for quadruplets pregnancies [1]

Respondents to the MOST Medical Birth survey reported higher averages for their multiples:

- 36 weeks for twins
- 33.1 weeks for triplets
- 31.3 weeks for quadruplets
- 29.7 weeks for quintuplets
- 29.3 weeks for sextuplets

Most perinatologists who have extensive experience with higher-order multiple pregnancies agree that your **goal** is to reach a gestational age of:

- **38 weeks for twins**
- **35-36 weeks triplets**
- **33-34 weeks for quadruplets and quintuplets**

The outcome of higher-order multiples depends on many factors. MOST has worked with almost 20,000 families since 1987 and the majority of expectant mothers of triplets and quadruplets who have contacted MOST have delivered healthy, albeit preterm babies. Even many higher-order multiples of quintuplets and sextuplets have had very good outcomes.

The most important factors are the number of babies involved in the pregnancy, the level of prematurity at birth, and the infant birth weights. The more babies involved, of course, the greater the risk, but the longer the gestation, the greater the chance for not just survival but also good health. Also, babies born at a longer gestation have a smaller possibility of long-term challenges associated with prematurity. Infants born more prematurely face a greater likelihood of complications.

The risk of perinatal loss (loss prior to or at birth) is higher for multiple gestation pregnancies than single gestation pregnancies. This risk decreases greatly as the pregnancy approaches 32 weeks gestation and beyond. The weeks between 18 and 23 weeks gestation are very critical to having the most successful outcome. During these weeks in particular, do not hesitate to call your health care provider with concerns and questions.

> If a higher-order multiple pregnancy is managed by a perinatologist or specialist who has significant experience with higher-order multiple pregnancies, the outcome is often much better than the average gestation for triplets, quadruplet and higher-order multiple births.

In addition, the quality of care in the NICU is an important factor in having a healthy outcome. Chapter 2 has information about picking a Neonatal Intensive Care Unit (NICU). When choosing a primary care physician for a higher-order pregnancy, ask about the provider's hospital affiliations. Inquire about hospital NICU survival statistics as well as how much experience the unit has caring for preterm higher-order multiple birth infants.

Early ultrasounds that show each baby being similar in size to that of a singleton and to each other also improves the probability of a positive outcome for these pregnancies. Later, when a level II sonogram (also called a comprehensive sonogram) done around 18 weeks gestation, reveals that each baby is still the same size as a singleton at that gestation and is healthy and free of obvious congenital abnormalities, the odds continue to improve. Another positive indicator is if the mother does not encounter any significant challenges between 18 to 24 weeks gestation, such as infection, spotting, leaking amniotic fluid or preterm labor.

> Of triplet pregnancies, 98% of all babies born after 28 weeks gestation survive!

Unfortunately, this is not the case for every pregnancy and just as in a singleton non-high-risk pregnancy unexplained losses can occur at any time. The risk of long-term complications decrease greatly as the pregnancy approaches and then exceeds the average gestation for the number of multiples carried. Be sure, throughout your pregnancy, to share your questions and concerns with your doctor so that he or she can support and advise you most appropriately.

Fraternal versus Identical: About Multiple Birth Zygosity

"My husband had a weird dream after we found out we were pregnant but before we knew there were three. Now you are going to think I totally made this up, but it is true. He dreamt that he was giving three babies a bath in a bathtub but then realized he did not know which one was which! A few weeks later we found out we were having triplets and three weeks after that we found out they were almost certainly identical. How weird is that?"

Fraternal (not identical) multiples are the most common zygosity (type of twinning) in higher-order multiples. About 80% of triplets or more, and an even higher percentage when triplets or more are conceived using fertility treatments, are fraternal. If your multiples are fraternal that means they do not share a placenta or an amniotic sac (the membrane that surrounds the fetus). Dizygotic (fraternal twins), trizygotic (fraternal triplets), tetrazygotic (fraternal quadruplets), or pentazygotic (fraternal quintuplets) multiples occur when two or more embryos implant from separate fertilized eggs and can result in the same or different genders. Although the placenta of fraternal multiples may appear to fuse as the pregnancy progresses due to proximity, fraternal multiples do not "share" a placenta or amniotic sac. The DNA of fraternal multiples could be as similar or different as any other genetic siblings.

Identical multiples (monozygotic) are the result of a single fertilized egg splitting into 2, 3, 4 or more babies and will result in same gender multiples who share nearly identical DNA. Fewer than 20% of higher-order pregnancies involve identical multiples. The babies may appear in separate distinct sacs and with separate placentas, or they may share the same placenta (monochorionic: meaning one chorion or placenta). A small percentage of monochorionic multiples may also share the same amniotic sac (monoamniotic).

In higher-order multiples zygosity types can also occur in a wide variety of combinations. For example, triplets can consist of two identical (monozygotic) multiples of the same gender and one fraternal (dizygotic) multiple of the same or a different gender. Quadruplets could consist of a set of identical triplets (monozygotic) with a fraternal (dizygotic) sibling. Respondents to the MOST Medical Birth survey indicated the following zygosity types for their multiple birth pregnancies:

Type of Conception	All Fraternal	Combination Fraternal & Identical	All Identical	Unknown
Spontaneous (no fertility treatments)	36.2%	35.0%	16.9%	11.9%
Fertility Medications	89.2%	6.6%	0.1%	4.1%
ART Conception	86.5%	9.2%	0.6%	3.7%

Monoamniotic gestations are extremely rare and can present some additional risks such as cord entanglement and conjoining. If one monochorionic multiple is lost early in the first trimester the other identical multiple is at a greater risk of being miscarried as well. The greatest risk in a mono-chorionic/amniotic pregnancy is Twin-to-Twin Transfusion Syndrome (TTTS), but luckily this is a rare condition. These situations can be managed through vigilant monitoring, and expectant parents should note that these complications are extremely rare in higher-order multiples. [See chapter 4 for more information on TTTS.] Once a doctor sees that there is a possibility of identicals, some couples are counseled to reduce or terminate their pregnancy. Speaking with a physician who has managed many higher order multiple pregnancies with at least one set of identicals before making a decision about reducing/terminating the pregnancy is extremely important. In most of these pregnancies the babies are carried successfully without a reduction.

To determine zygosity your doctor may look for separate and distinct sacs as well as separate and distinct placentas for each baby. Often early sonograms between 8-12 weeks can determine zygosity as well as during the comprehensive ultrasound (or sonogram) usually done between 12-18 weeks gestation. Unfortunately, this method can only confirm identical multiples when more than one infant shares a placenta or amniotic sac. Because identical multiples can also appear separated, monozygosity cannot be ruled out if separate sacs and placentas are seen. Unless zygosity is confirmed through a shared amniotic sac or placenta (not just a merged placenta which can sometime happen with fraternal multiples), the only definitive way to know zygosity is to test the placentas at the time of delivery or to have DNA testing for each child after birth.

Fetal Reductions

"My heart feels we were given this gift for a reason, and reducing is not an option for me, but being told over and over that a reduction is the safest thing to do really takes a toll. Hearing from other families is such an inspiration and makes me feel so much better."

"Every parent of quintuplets has been faced with this decision. It did not seem to me as if there was any best decision. We each have to decide. 'What could my heart live with at the end of the day' is what I say."

A Multifetal Pregnancy Reduction (MFPR) is a procedure that reduces the number of fetuses or embryos, depending on the gestation of the pregnancy, to increase the likelihood of a successful pregnancy. Another term often used is a selective reduction. This is a reduction of one or more fetuses or embryos due to serious anomalies. Many parents expecting triplets, quadruplets, or more will face the decision whether or not to have a multifetal pregnancy reduction. The decision is a very personal one. Unfortunately the person who initially suggests that you should consider a reduction *is often not experienced* in the care and management of a high-risk pregnancy and therefore not the appropriate person to be offering this type of medical advice. Expectant parents have had experiences where the ultrasound technician, the nurse at the fertility clinic or even the secretary told them they *need* to reduce. Sometimes the doctor at the fertility clinic recommends reduction. Please keep in mind that his or her area of expertise is helping a woman become pregnant and not in caring for a pregnant woman and her babies during the pregnancy. The most appropriate doctor to advise you is a perinatologist with much experience handling higher-order multiple pregnancies and better than average gestational outcomes. This is especially true for women carrying 4 or more babies. [See Table 1 of Dr. Elliott's article "Managing Higher-Order Multiple Pregnancies" in Chapter 3 of this book.]

If a couple believes that a reduction is in the best interest of their family, the procedure is usually performed as an outpatient early in the pregnancy between 7 and 14 weeks gestation. Often a CVS (chorionic villus sampling) is performed to determine if there are chromosomal abnormalities and allow for reduction of those fetuses. Guided by ultrasound through either the abdomen or vagina, a needle is inserted into the fetus, and potassium chloride is injected into the fetus to stop the heart. Since the fetus is very small it is usually absorbed by the mother's body as the pregnancy progresses. There are generally no remnants visible at delivery. The two primary goals of an MFPR are:

1. To achieve a longer pregnancy gestation
2. To achieve higher infant birth weights

The risks associated with an MFPR include:

- Miscarriage of one or more of the remaining fetuses
- Fetal/intrauterine growth restriction (IUGR) of the remaining fetuses
- Preterm premature rupture of the membranes (PPROM)
- Preterm labor
- Infection

A reduction in a triplet pregnancy is generally not considered medically necessary; however, your medical history and health may indicate a reduction is the safest route for you and your babies. The American College of Obstetricians and Gynecologists (ACOG) states the following about multifetal reduction and selective fetal termination:

Higher-order multiple gestations create a medical and ethical dilemma. If a pregnancy with 4 or more fetuses is continued, the probability is high that not all fetuses will survive intact [without serious medical complications] and that the woman will experience morbidity [health complications]. However, fetal reduction to triplets or twin gestations is associated with a significant risk of losing either another fetus or the whole pregnancy. [Studies have shown the risk of loss at 11.7% and the risk of a very premature delivery, between 25 and 28 weeks gestation, at 4.5% for pregnancies involving a reduction.] Note: this risk increased further with each additional fetus. Most studies have concluded that the risks associated with a quadruplet or higher pregnancy clearly outweigh the risks associated with fetal reduction. [4]

Dr. Victor R. Klein, a perinatologist at North Shore University Hospital in New York, has delivered hundreds of higher-order multiple pregnancies, and here is what he recommends:

"Several individual factors also lead to the recommendation for a reduction based on number of fetuses. Does the mother have medical issues that might adversely affect a successful outcome for a higher-order multiple gestation? Is the mother at high-risk for preterm delivery based on uterine factors? While some physicians recommend reductions for any pregnancy greater than twins, others never recommend reduction. Individualized counseling is most important when the issue of reduction is considered."

Included in this book in chapter 3 is an article by Dr. John Elliott who has also delivered many quadruplet and above pregnancies, and we encourage all families facing this decision to please read that article before deciding if a fetal reduction is appropriate for them.

Dealing with the decision of whether or not to undergo multifetal pregnancy reduction can be a traumatic experience. Couples who have invested a great deal of time, money, energy and emotion in pursuing a pregnancy are often unprepared to make this decision. Undergoing professional or spiritual counseling prior to the procedure is usually helpful to couples considering multifetal reduction. Both partners need to be comfortable with their decision and may need emotional support prior to, and immediately following, the procedure. Many parents report not feeling the full emotional affect until the remaining babies are born or even up to one year after delivery. A small percentage of parents experience some lingering feelings of sadness or guilt for a couple of years, but most families (both parents and children) are generally well adjusted when evaluated a few years after the procedure. To date no clear consensus exists on whether or how to tell the remaining children about the procedure as they grow.

MOST recommends that any parent considering a multifetal reduction consult with a Maternal-Fetal Medicine Specialist (MFMS or Perinatologist) experienced in working with multiple-birth pregnancies prior to making a decision. [Expectant parents can contact MOST for more information about experienced perinatologists who would be qualified to counsel them on this issue.] MOST also recommends that parents seek both pre-procedure and, if the procedure is performed, post-procedure counseling. In addition, parents who have decided to undergo the procedure should work only with a facility and medical professionals with substantial experience performing this exact procedure to minimize the risk of complications or loss because of the reduction. Ask the facility and professionals what their pregnancy loss rate is for reductions performed on pregnancies such as yours. Ask in particular what their pregnancy loss rate is between 18 and 23 weeks: the most tentative time in a higher-order multiple pregnancy. This is a period not reflected in the medical literature since the focus is often on the first 4 weeks post procedure (up to 18 weeks) and then live births (after 23 weeks).

A pregnancy that has been reduced is still a high-risk pregnancy.

References

(1)   Martin JA, Hamilton BE, Ventura SJ, et al. Births: Final data for 2009. National vital statistics reports; vol 60 no 1. Hyattsville, MD: National Center for Health Statistics. 2011. http://www.cdc.gov/nchs/data/nvsr/nvsr60/nvsr60_01.pdf (accessed June 21, 2012).

(2)   Centers for Disease Control and Prevention, American Society for Reproductive Medicine, Society for Assisted Reproductive Technology. 2009 Assisted Reproductive Technology Success Rates: National Summary and Fertility Clinic Reports. Atlanta: U.S. Department of Health and Human Services; 2011. http://www.cdc.gov/art/ART2009/PDF/01_ARTSuccessRates09-FM.pdf (accessed June 22, 2012).

(3)   Hoyert, D L, and et al. "Annual Summary of Vital Statistics: 2004." Pediatrics 117, no. 1 (January 2006): 168-183.

(4)   American College of Obstetricians and Gynecologists. "Multiple Gestation: Complicated Twin, Triplet, and Higher-order Multifetal Pregnancy." *ACOG Practice Bulletin* 56, no. 104 (2004): 869-883.

Resources

Incidence of Multiples

- RESOLVE also offers information about multiples titled: *Avoiding Multiples Births in IVF:* www.resolve.org/family-building-options/avoiding-multiple-births-in-ivf.html

- MOST FAQs on this topic: www.MOSTonline.org/faq_friends.htm

- Odds of having multiples: www.MOSTonline.org/facts_outsideresources.htm

Identical Twin and Twin-to-Twin Transfusion Syndrome

- For more information on identical twin gestations visit: www.monoamniotic.org

- Twin-To-Twin Transfusion Syndrome Foundation is solely dedicated to providing immediate and lifesaving educational, emotional and financial support to families, medical professionals and other caregivers before, during and after a diagnosis of Twin-to-Twin Transfusion Syndrome: www.tttsfoundation.org/

- The Mom 2 Many website offers more detailed information on zygosity testing: www.mom2many.com/dna.htm

Pregnancy Reduction/ Selective Reduction

- ACOG statement on Multifetal Pregnancy Reductions: www.acog.org/Resources_And_Publications/Committee_Opinions/Committee_on_Ethics/Multifetal_Pregnancy_Reduction

- American Society for Reproductive Medicine's report on Multifetal Pregnancy Reduction (PDF): www.asrm.org/topics/detail.aspx?id=1610

- PeaceHealth's "Should I consider a multifetal pregnancy reduction?": www.peacehealth.org/xhtml/content/decisionpoint/tn10007.html

- Check the MOST Medical News page for recent research studies on this health topic: http://www.mostonline.org/research.htm

- Selective Reduction Loss Support is an online email group for parents who undergo a selective reduction: http://health.groups.yahoo.com/group/SelectiveReductionLossSupport/

- MOST also has resource volunteers available for families considering a selective reduction: www.mostonline.org/volunteers.htm

Fertility Treatment

- Society for Assisted Reproductive Technology provides information on reproductive technologies such as in-vitro fertilization, frozen embryos, ovarian stimulation and more: www.sart.org/detail.aspx?id=1867

- MOST Recommendations on the Responsible Use of Fertility Treatments (PDF): www.MOSTonline.org/FertilityTreatmentsandMultiples.pdf

- Visit the MOST Supertwins Statistics page to learn more about multiple birth complications: www.MOSTonline.org/facts.htm

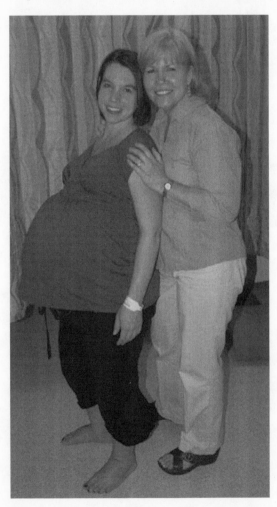

Chapter 2: Proactive Pregnancies

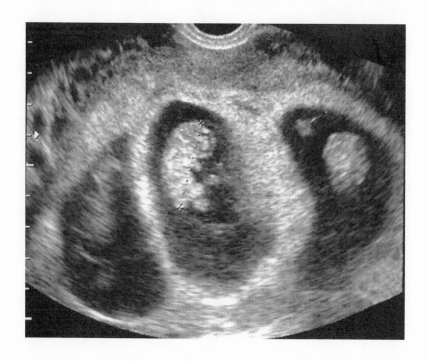

"In case you have not already, I think it is very important to also get advice from a doctor who has successfully delivered many triplets or more. Some people have even relocated to be near a top doctor. Our doctor was really helpful about explaining the pros and cons then letting us make the decision. These are the doctors who can truly tell you the statistics and help you through it. You need a doctor who will support you."

"I was surprised that not all of the doctors in the group were on the same page. Each of them suggested different supplements, medications and activity levels throughout my pregnancy."

hat does it mean to have a **proactive** pregnancy? It means that you and your supporters (husband, significant other, other family and friends) search, read and ask questions. Sometimes it means making tough choices (changing doctors, relocating for care, etc.); sometimes it means preparing yourself and family for what will come (NICU, caring for 2, 3 or more babies). Through the years we have found that the parents who were proactive during pregnancy had an overall better pregnancy, delivery and NICU course. This does not mean that they had no pregnancy complications, delivered at 38 weeks, faced no time in the NICU or hired a nanny for each child. It means that these parents gathered knowledge (information and experience) about this pregnancy, made informed decisions, found resources, and, as best they could, prepared for having multiple babies at home!

This chapter covers important information about choosing your doctor and hospital and other information about having a proactive pregnancy. Hopefully the best choice of doctor will give you the best choice of hospital as well. Some women think that their pregnancy will not have complications or problems, but the vast majority of higher-order multiple pregnancies and many twin pregnancies have some type of complications ranging from mild to severe. You want the best doctor with the most experience and best outcomes caring for you and your babies if at all possible. Some mothers have changed doctors as late as 20+ weeks into their pregnancy to receive the best care.

Choosing Your Doctors

Finding the right physician for a high-risk pregnancy (all higher-order pregnancies and many twin pregnancies are high-risk) is very important. After all your babies' lives and yours are involved. There are three types of physicians who can care for you and the babies.

- General Obstetrician (OB-GYN) – may or may not be board certified
- High-Risk Specialist – an OB-GYN who has additional training in high-risk pregnancies
- Perinatologist or Maternal-Fetal Medicine (MFM) Specialist – an OB-GYN who has completed 2 to 3 years of a Maternal-Fetal Medicine fellowship after completing 4 years of an Obstetrics and Gynecology residency

Many women are reluctant to change health care providers even if their doctor has not delivered triplets within the past few years. Some of their reasons include:

- Comfortable with physician
- Loyalty to physician
- Trust in physician
- Convenience/proximity of practice
- Insurance restrictions
- Delivery at local hospital
- Delivered other children with no problems
- Physician says he can handle this pregnancy
- Physician says he has delivered many twins
- Physician "helped me get pregnant after years of infertility"

- Do not want to hurt the physician's feelings
- Practice treats the pregnant mother "special" because they rarely get to deliver triplets or more

Some doctors would love to have you as a patient for the prestige and the possible media attention would be good for their practice. However, you need to find the best doctor and best hospital to have the healthiest babies. You are your babies' most important advocate. Although you may not feel comfortable changing doctors, you need to be cared for by the best doctor for your babies.

MOST's Position: MOST strongly recommends an expectant mother of high risk twins, and all expectant mothers of triplets, quadruplets, quintuplets or more be under the primary care of a board certified Perinatologist/MFM during pregnancy.

Although changing doctors does not guarantee you will have healthy babies, by seeing an MFMS who has experience with high-risk twin, triplet and quadruplet pregnancies you have greatly increased your chances of having the healthiest babies possible.

The American College of Obstetricians and Gynecologists (ACOG) does consider a higher-order multiple pregnancy high-risk but gives no definite regulations stating that a Maternal-Fetal Medicine Specialist must oversee a triplet or more pregnancy. An MFMS is an obstetric sub-specialist concerned with the care of the mother and fetus who are at a higher than normal risk of complications. These specialists are much more experienced managing a complicated higher-order multiple pregnancy. Even within the field of perinatology there are some physicians who have considerably more experience providing care and achieving better than average outcomes for mothers expecting higher-order multiples.

High-Risk Pregnancy Analogies

Would you feel comfortable in these situations?

1. You get on a plane and meet the pilot, a very pleasant man. He is so excited today since this is his very first flight! He welcomes you enthusiastically and he tells you how much he will remember you as his very first passenger.

2. You are ready to buy a new car; you check Consumer Reports™, ask your friends and even strangers, look around to see what is available and buy what you consider the best car on the market. A short time later you find that your needs in a car have changed. To see if another car on the market better suits your present needs, you go through the same steps of checking Consumer Reports™, asking friends for recommendations etc. Even if the salesperson for the car you previously purchased is a friend and a good person, the cars he sells do not have what you need now. Do you still buy a car from him anyway?

3. Your job has transferred you from sunny, flat Florida to the snowy mountains of Colorado, and you do not know many people who live in Colorado. You can talk with others who have the information you need, but you decide not to ask anyone, using your knowledge of Florida to figure out Colorado instead.

How to Find a Maternal-Fetal Medicine Specialist

Ask your obstetrician to see which MFM Specialist he recommends. Be sure to ask for two names in case one is not available.

1. Call or check the website of a university hospital in your area. Find out if they have a Maternal-Fetal Medicine Department and which physicians are affiliated. Ask those physicians how many triplet or more pregnancies they have delivered in the past three years.

2. Call a hospital with a Level III NICU in the area if available.

3. Ask labor and delivery nurses from the larger local hospitals who they would go to for care if they were expecting triplets or more or were expecting high-risk twins.

4. Locate a local triplet plus support group and ask the mothers who they used/liked. Find out the gestation and outcome they achieved. Contact MOST to help locate a group near you.

Not All Maternal-Fetal Medicine Specialists are Alike

1. Some physicians are more proactive, anticipating problems before they occur, while some physicians are more reactive, only reacting to problems once they occur.

2. Some physicians do not use any interventions or medications until babies are deemed viable (around 23-24 weeks).

3. The American College of Obstetricians and Gynecologists (ACOG) sets no definite guidelines on how to handle a higher-order multiple or other high-risk pregnancy which is why experience is critical.

Each pregnancy has its own challenges (none for a few lucky families!) and therefore must be addressed individually. You and your spouse need to discuss with each other how aggressive you want to be with this pregnancy. Some couples feel that they tried so hard to get pregnant they will do ANYTHING to maintain the pregnancy, while others feel nature will do what is best. Would you like a doctor who is going to be as proactive in sustaining your pregnancy as you are?

Suggested Interview Questions for both Obstetricians and MFMS

Using a small spiral notebook start a pregnancy data book. Write down your concerns and questions for your doctor(s). Take it to all your appointments and let your doctor know you have a few questions. If you see several doctors within the same group, ask each the same questions. In addition, you will want to ask your OB-GYN and MFMS (if you see both) the same questions to see if they have the same pregnancy management plan.

Write down the answers before you leave the office. You may want to keep it by your bed so you can write in it at night when questions and concerns seem to come up! Another section of the notebook can be a "To Do List" and another to use

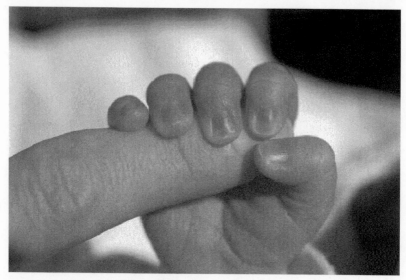

as a journal with your thoughts and emotions. This book can be a valuable way to be an informed patient as well as serve as a memory of these times and a source of information for questions asked later by health care providers, insurance companies, medical and educational intake forms or other mothers you may help.

1. Are you a Maternal-Fetal Medicine Specialist?

2. If not, will you be consulting with one or co-managing my pregnancy with one? Will you be my primary doctor managing my care or will you be sharing care with others in your group? Do you all follow the same protocols? If I have a question or concern should I ask for you?

3. How often will I need to have appointments? Do you have a management plan or schedule for seeing your high-risk twin, or your triplet or more patients?

4. How often will I need to see the specialist and my regular OB-GYN?

5. Under what, if any, circumstances will my care be transferred to this specialist?

6. How many sets of triplets, quadruplets, etc. have you personally managed/delivered within the past two to three years? *Note that this question is to the doctor alone: not his practice or the hospital.*

7. What is your average gestation with pregnancies involving as many babies as mine? MOST's average is 33.3 weeks for triplets and 32 weeks for quadruplets.. The national average for triplets is also 31.9 weeks and quadruplet pregnancies average 29.5 weeks.[5] (This is information the physician should know and be willing to share.)

8. How far will you let my pregnancy progress? (How does this answer compare to the optimum goals stated in the section on Average Gestations earlier in this book? A pregnancy allowed to continue past those goals may have a higher increase of complications for the babies and the mother.) What will be my absolute long-term goal? (Circle that date on your calendar!)

9. Will you be proactive in sustaining my pregnancy if I develop complications, such as preterm labor, before the babies are deemed viable outside the womb (usually around 23 weeks)?

10. How aggressive will you be about preventing or treating preterm labor? What medications, procedures or therapies will you consider to manage any contractions?

11. What hospital(s) can you admit to? Is the MFMS also at this hospital?

12. Does this hospital have a Level III NICU? Are babies EVER transferred out of this hospital for any reason?

13. If this hospital does not have a Level III NICU, and one or more of the babies need to be transferred, where will they be transferred to and how will I see them? Can I deliver at that hospital?

14. What are your hours and how can I contact you after hours? If you share call, how does that work? Do you usually deliver your patients?

15. What other physicians take calls for your patients? Will they follow your treatment plan? If I have to go to the hospital in an emergency, who should be called: you or the MFMS?

16. If I ever have to go to the hospital on an emergency basis can I request that only you be allowed to give me a vaginal internal exam (not another attending, resident, nurse, medical student)?

17. If another attending may examine me should I meet with this doctor at some point early in my pregnancy?

Advocating for Your Babies

- Be assertive, ask questions and seek a second opinion if you are not comfortable with anything or anyone.

- Be informed: READ, ASK and RESEARCH

  o Read related materials recommended at the end of each of these chapters, material from your doctor, and the MOST website.

  o Ask if something is concerning you. If something is unclear or you thought that you understood something but it is no longer clear, be sure to ask your doctor to explain it again for you.

  o Research by learning the facts and statistics. Read recommended (and reviewed) links from the MOST website: ww.MOSTonline.org

- As the parent you need to be the ultimate advocate for your babies.

- Some communities do not have a Maternal-Fetal Specialist accessible. If this is your situation:

  o Demand, respectfully, that your regular OB-GYN consult a MFMS to co-manage your pregnancy.

  o Consider relocating to an area with MFM Specialists available and who have had more experience with pregnancies similar to yours. Many women have relocated for care quite successfully and MOST can offer information and support if this is appropriate for you.

MFM Specialists recognize that many OB-GYNs are qualified by training and experience to manage complicated pregnancies, so they are usually willing to provide consultations and co-management especially when location or finances prevent the pregnant mother from relocating or changing providers. In some areas where the number of MFM providers is limited the MFMS are usually experienced in managing higher-order multiple pregnancies for those who live a great distance from their practice. They can provide advice and recommendations on how best to approach this situation. Not all MFMS will do this though, so if you have a concern about this, please call the MOST office.

Choosing a Hospital for Delivery

Finding the right hospital to deliver your babies, who will in all likelihood be preterm, is just as important as finding the right physician for your high-risk pregnancy. The best hospital may not be the closest. A family expecting triplets or more should very seriously check out available hospitals. The mother may need to relocate closer to the right hospital before complications occur: preferably before 18-20 weeks gestation. Some inconvenience in the short-term while pregnant can prevent long-term problems later in the pregnancy, the delivery and the health of your babies. You may be asking two different doctors these questions and it is important to know the answers from each one. (Some questions are similar to those in the section above.)

Questions to Ask Your OB-GYN or MFM Physician:

1. Where are you planning to deliver my babies?

2. Does the hospital have a Level III Nursery?

3. When was the last time higher-order multiples were born there? What was the outcome? When was the last time you delivered triplets (or more) at this hospital?

4. How many Level III NICU beds do they have?

5. What is the likelihood that one or more of the babies would need to be transferred?

6. Where would they be transferred?

7. If they have to be transferred, why should I not deliver there instead so I will not be separated from the babies?

8. At what week gestation, if any, would you feel comfortable transferring me to a hospital with a Level II NICU nursery to deliver?

Types of Neonatal Intensive Care Units (NICU)

1. **Level I: Basic Neonatal Care Nursery**
   1. Minimum requirement for any facility that provides inpatient maternity care.
   2. Must have equipment and personnel to perform neonatal resuscitation, evaluate healthy newborns, provide postnatal care and stabilize ill newborns until they can be transferred to another facility.

2. **Level II: Specialty Care Nursery**
   1. Can provide care to infants who are moderately ill with problems that are expected to resolve quickly, such as a short-term need for oxygen, IV fluids or feeding tubes.

2. Can resuscitate and stabilize a preterm and/or ill infant before transfer to a different facility that can provide Level III care.

3. Can provide care to newborns who are recovering from a serious illness previously treated in a Level III NICU Nursery.

3. **Level III: Sub-specialty Neonatal Intensive Care Nursery**

1. Can care for premature newborns or newborns that are critically ill or require surgical intervention.

2. Must be capable of providing complex, multi-system life support for an indefinite period.

3. Must be capable of providing mechanical ventilation and invasive cardiovascular monitoring or care of a similar nature. Surgical specialists are available.

There are four levels of Level III NICU nurseries. At Level IIIA (the lowest level), the hospital or state restricts the mechanical ventilation type or duration. The highest level, Level IIID, has no restrictions on ventilation use and is the only level that can provide cardiopulmonary bypass and/or ECMO (heart lung bypass machines) for medical conditions.

Find out where the nearest Level III NICU is located and whether it is Level III A/B/C/D. Know how your babies would get there from the hospital your physician plans to use for delivery if needed. Transferring may delay treatment, which could lead to serious complications, and may even be the difference between life and death.

What to Look for in a Level III NICU

Below are different aspects of the NICU you will want to consider. Of course, not everyone has a choice of which NICU their babies will go to; however, when you visit the NICU prior to delivery these areas are important to note. If you do have a choice use this list to help guide your decision on where to deliver.

- **Size** - Learn about the total number of preemies treated at this facility or how many infants are treated in their NICU each year. Larger programs have more expertise and a greater depth of resources. With

50

multiples, the NICU needs to have enough "Level III beds" for all of them. Some hospitals have only a few ventilators available for neonates (preemies). The staff at larger hospitals is more likely to have experience with multiples and possible complications of a preterm infants. Beware of Community Hospitals claiming to have Level III nurseries without the actual credentials.

- **Around the clock care** - Is a Neonatologist (or a Pediatric Hospitalist or Neonatal Nurse Practitioner) on site 24 hours a day? On-call or available is not good enough. The specialist must be in the hospital because just a few seconds could be the difference between life and death. Are neonatal nurse practitioners on site 24 hours a day? Are several respiratory therapists on site 24 hours a day?

- **Respiratory care** - Respiratory problems affect 40 to 50 percent of babies born before 32 weeks. Some will require a ventilator. Many multiples are born before 32 weeks and some will require a ventilator or other respiratory treatments. Respiratory therapies such as high-frequency ventilation and surfactant therapy must be available. Respiratory Distress Syndrome (RDS) is the most common complication of prematurity and is caused by underdeveloped lungs, which lack sufficient surfactant (a fatty substance) to keep the lungs open. Artificial surfactant is placed directly into the lungs of a premature infant via a tube immediately after delivery. Ask if surfactant is routinely given in the delivery room or if they wait until the baby is transferred to the NICU. Some neonatologists believe that surfactant given in the delivery room is beneficial. Due to the use of surfactant, nearly 90 percent of babies who develop RDS now survive.

- **Environmental stimulation** - Preemies can be very sensitive to touch, sound, bright light and other forms of stimulation. The NICU should have procedures to minimize light and sound. Some NICU have certain types of lighting to minimize bright lights. Soundproofing and special flooring help eliminate noise. Even the room arrangement is important as big rooms are noisier than private rooms or pods, and the location of the nursing desks make a difference in the noise level for babies nearby.

- **A pharmacy specifically for preparing infant prescriptions** - Neonatal doses are very different from adult doses. A special pharmacy or a pharmacist that specializes in neonatal medications is much safer and less likely to make mistakes than a pharmacy or pharmacist that provides for the whole hospital.

- **Family centered care focused on priorities and choices of families** - The following questions will help you find out what is available for you while your babies are in the NICU/hospital.

    1. Does the NICU allow unlimited parental visiting privileges or sleeping accommodations? Are the visiting hours adequate for families with several babies in NICU? Can visiting hours be extended to meet the needs of multiple birth families?

    2. Can the babies be situated near each other when medically possible?

    3. Will the NICU make available a coordinator for your family to serve as a liaison between staff and parents, so you can meet all the doctors involved in each of your babies' care?

    4. Does the hospital have a parent support person for families with multiples?

    5. Do professionals treat the babies as a group or as individuals and refer to them by name? Can they give some examples of how the hospital achieves this?

    6. Does the staff encourage you to do newborn care activities like give baths, change diapers, help with tube feedings?

    7. Will a high-risk clinic be available to follow up on the babies' progress after discharge? If not, will someone coordinate

discharge needs, services, and referrals to a high-risk clinic or developmental center prior to discharge?

8. Will you be provided with a list of resources and are books available?

9. Does the staff support and encourage breastfeeding multiples? Are mothers instructed on nursing at the breast or just encouraged to use a breast pump? Does the hospital have an in-house lactation consultant and lactation room in the NICU? Does she have experience with higher-order multiples? Will you have an opportunity to have a supervised breastfeeding experience at the breast at least three times with each of your babies prior to discharge?

10. Will the staff color code your newborn items and breast milk?

11. Will you be given information on where to find preemie clothes, diapers, baby books for premature infants, etc.? Are any items available in the hospital gift shop?

12. Will you be instructed on preemie behavior for their gestation while in the NICU and prior to discharge (i.e., more fussy, startles easy, signs of stress, etc.)?

13. Are discharged babies allowed back when parents visit remaining hospitalized babies?

14. Is the staff supportive when parents cannot return to visit hospitalized infants (i.e., when no one is available to care for discharged babies or siblings)?

15. Are parents expecting multiple births encouraged to tour the NICU prior to the birth of their babies?

16. Does the hospital have support for siblings such as special visiting times, sibling room or hospital tour that includes the NICU? These should be available to parents and siblings before

the birth of multiples. Is sibling support available for older children as well?

17. Will you be able to take any parenting classes after delivery that you may have missed because you were on bedrest prior to delivery?

- **Guidelines for unnecessary tests** - There are tests that your babies will need; however, some tests can be eliminated, delayed or combined. The NICU staff should strive to reduce the number of tests. Fewer tests produce less stress for the babies and you. How does the NICU limit or bundle testing? Do they have guidelines for reducing or eliminating unnecessary testing?

- **Nutritional care** - Providing breast milk for your babies is recommended if possible, and having access to lactation consultants can be very beneficial. Is there a milk bank available if you are unable to provide enough breast milk? Is there a special team of professionals responsible for evaluating the nutritional needs of each baby?

- **Surgical care and bedside surgery** - Because moving a fragile premature infant is a high-risk task, it should be done only in extreme emergencies. Certain abdominal and bowel surgeries, as well as those to correct severe respiratory problems, can often be done at the bedside in the NICU. Special cabling in the unit allows the surgical team to perform surgeries and transmit EEG, ultrasound and echocardiogram data to pediatric sub-specialists in other parts of the hospital for real-time interpretation. Bedside procedures have been proven to produce better results because the newborns have more positive outcomes than those who are moved. These procedures are also less costly since there are no additional charges for surgical suites and recovery rooms. Some surgeries may need to be done outside of the NICU.

- **Preparation for NICU discharge for parents and other caregivers -**
  - When does the hospital start preparing parents for discharge? How do they do this? Is there a plan or checklist?
  - Does the NICU provide or require CPR training for family and other caregivers? Is there a fee?
  - Is there a Family Care Coordinator to help answer questions you may have?
  - What parenting classes are available? Are there any that are multiple birth specific?
  - Do you have an opportunity to room-in prior to discharge?
  - Is there an NICU support group for parents with infant(s) in the NICU?
  - Is an infant car seat check done? (Usually required)
  - Is instruction given on infection control at home (proper hand washing, sanitizing items, etc.)?
  - Is an appointment for developmental follow-up scheduled before discharge?
  - What immunizations/vaccines are generally given prior to discharge?
  - If you plan to have your son(s) circumcised, who will coordinate this with our OB-GYN prior to discharge? When is this typically done?

- **Ongoing Research** - The neonatal field is constantly changing and improving at a rapid pace. If your NICU conducts research, they probably use the most up-to-date methods, so ask if your hospital does research. Just because the NICU does not conduct research does not mean they are out of date. Using up-to-date methods and techniques of treatment could prevent lasting disabilities.

How to Find a Good Level III Neonatal Center or NICU

- Ask your Maternal-Fetal Medicine Specialist or OB-GYN

- If you already have a pediatrician or pediatric primary health care provider be sure to ask for his/her opinion.

- Call or check the website of a university hospital in your area to find out if they have a neonatal department. Be sure to check the website in detail to see what they offer.

- Ask nurses from local hospitals where they would recommend going if they were expecting high-risk twins, or triplets or more.

Relocating for Care

"The moms on the MOST forums showed me it was possible to have quads and from them I learned of Dr. Elliott. Even if you do not go to him to be under his care, he is worth calling and speaking to. He can even work as a consult to your doctors. I went to 30 weeks and had 4 healthy beautiful babies!"

"I thought I would deliver in the city where I live. It has a Level III NICU and perinatologists. However, after we spoke with the perinatologists, my husband and I realized they had no positive experience with quadruplets and not very many even with triplets. I ended up moving at week 20 to obtain care elsewhere. This was a very difficult decision in so many ways. My home, 2-year-old and friends were left behind while I went to a place where I did not know anyone. However, this was the best decision we made. Although I was far from friends and family, I ended up delivering the healthiest four babies I could due to the medical care I received from my new doctors and nurses. It was worth the price. Looking at the big picture, 12 weeks was just a short period of time. The babies deserved to be the healthiest they could be; and my toddler deserved the healthiest siblings I could give her."

Some mothers expecting higher-order multiples consider the option of relocating for prenatal care during their pregnancies. While relocating can be challenging for a family, this option is one worth considering should a mother live in an area where she does not have access to health care providers with the necessary skills and experience working with higher-order multiple pregnancies or access to a hospital with the appropriate level of NICU care. For some families deciding to relocate is an easy decision as they realize the babies will have a better chance of being born healthy if they receive care elsewhere. For other families it is a more difficult decision to make due to finances, concern of the unknown or other siblings. If you feel that better care can be provided elsewhere, many insurance companies will cover the medical costs if your physicians support it. This may not be your local MFMS (because he may want to provide you care) but this could be your regular OB-GYN and/or your family physician along with the MFMS you are relocating to. Just remember that relocating may be an inconvenience for you, but it is only for a short time: a few months compared to your babies' whole lives. Like many other decisions you make during this pregnancy, relocation is a decision that needs to be made in the best interest of the babies.

Because of the logistical challenges of temporarily relocating during such a critical time, MOST offers families who are considering this option or who have decided to relocate for care information and resources as well as support from MOST Resource Volunteers who have experience with relocation during pregnancy. To request this information, contact the MOST office.

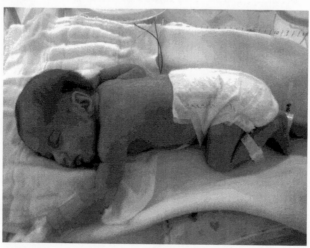

Special Note for Dads and Significant Others

"My husband was very gracious. He knew it was hard for me to feel so helpless. Every morning he would help me out of bed (especially near the end when I could not even adjust myself to sitting up in bed)."

Typically a spouse or partner will be the strongest supporter for the expectant mother during the pregnancy, especially if bedrest occurs, and during the hospitalization and delivery. Your strongest supporter could be a friend or family member. Please take these suggestions for your supporter, no matter who it is. If possible, the father should attend doctor visits and learn about this special pregnancy. Then he also can be proactive and help his wife have the most successful pregnancy.

Partners should be informed about medical information and updates since he may not be able to attend the appointments, especially if he has to care for the other children during these visits.

In addition to maintaining financial security, the partner may now have to assume additional and often unfamiliar roles that can increase stress upon the family. For example, the partner can help maintain the normal household routine, which helps other children in the family adjust. Hiring additional assistance for childcare and housework duties, if financially feasible, can help lighten the load.

Partners need time to spend with the mother even if they are just arranging a "date" while on bedrest with sitters taking responsibility for other children. This helps parents maintain communication and intimacy. Partners also will benefit from maintaining routines including time with friends and participating in hobbies on occasion. Even though some women on bedrest may resent his ability to engage in such excursions, these activities may allow him to "vent" and return to the family "rejuvenated."

Family and friends should make sure to take care of Dad too. If the partner starts feeling overwhelmed, he should be encouraged to talk with a professional, viewing it as a sign of strength not weakness, that he acknowledges such a need. In addition to caring for Dad, family and friends should also be aware that communication between core family members is critical. Expectant mothers, spouses/partners, and older children all need as much regular contact with each other as possible during this challenging time to help maintain their family unity.

Keeping Track of Concerns

As mentioned previously, expectant mother of multiples may want to get a small spiral notebook (ideally one with several sections) to keep track of all of your questions for your doctors, your to-do list, and key points you want to remember. It should be used similar to a journal. If you cannot find a sectioned book MOST suggests that you keep your to-do list in the back and questions for each of the doctors and your notes together in the front. The notebook would be a place to keep track of medications, tests and test results, supplements, questions, concerns and fears (rational and otherwise), etc. A second small, sectioned notebook can be used after the babies are born to keep track of similar questions for each individual baby or you can purchase a copy of the *NICU Notebook: A Parent's Journal.* Contact MOST for availability.

Be sure to bring your notebook to each of your doctor visits and write down your doctor's responses and instructions BEFORE leaving the office. It really is not uncommon for any expectant mother during the first few months of pregnancy to become forgetful due to hormones and many things to think about. It is important to write things down. It decreases the chances that you may recall the doctor saying one thing and your support person remembering it differently. You may still need some clarification in the future about what something meant and the notebook will help you remember what you want to clarify.

During the first few months, many expectant mothers have problems with insomnia due to fluctuating hormones and a million thoughts running through their heads when they are trying to sleep. If you get up during the night, you may find you are preoccupied with worries or unfinished details such as: Will all of the babies be okay? What if one looks like crazy Uncle Harry? Should we paint the room now or wait? Will 3 cribs fit into the room? Did the dry cleaning get picked up? Are we out of dog food? Should this occur, you may want to write down these thoughts so you can let go of them instead of having to remember them in the morning. Mothers pregnant with multiples can frequently feel stressed or anxious during their pregnancy, and this may be more common with mothers who undergo fertility treatment. If this sounds like you, you are not alone! Writing down your thoughts and feelings is one way to deal with this. Other ways include speaking with your doctors and nurses or connecting with other mothers of multiples to obtain support.

MOST offers an Infant Multiples booklet that you may want to order at about 26 weeks gestation. It will help answer questions of what is coming. The booklet is filled with pertinent information about the NICU, feeding, a grams-pounds weight conversion chart, feeding/diaper/medication charts, frequently asked questions, developmental milestones, Early Intervention, postpartum depression, choosing a pediatrician, and much, much more.

Care of Teeth and Gums

Taking care of your teeth and gums may help your babies! Studies indicate pregnant women with periodontal disease, an infection of the gums and other tissues that support the teeth, are more likely to have preterm, low-birth-weight babies. [6] Some studies also find that women with periodontal disease are at higher risk for preeclampsia. [7] Any infection, including periodontal infection, can cause contractions and preterm birth. Since a higher-order multiple pregnancy is high-risk, anything you can do to decrease your risk of a premature birth is helpful. A visit to the dentist will help you have the healthiest teeth and gums.

Gingivitis is the mildest form of periodontal disease. The hormones of pregnancy cause gum tissues to swell and increase the supply of blood to the gums so you may develop gingivitis. Gingivitis causes inflamed gums that bleed when you brush or floss your teeth. If this develops while you are pregnant, it is called pregnancy gingivitis. Gingivitis usually does not cause any problems. To help prevent gingivitis, brush and floss your teeth daily. Gingivitis, if untreated, can become worse and develop into periodontitis.

The best time for dental work is before you are pregnant; however, it is usually safe to have dental work, including x-rays, while pregnant. Ask you OB-GYN or perinatologist for their approval for any work beyond cleaning your teeth, and be sure to tell your dentist you are in a high-risk pregnancy. Ask for oral care suggestions now and if there is an oral rinse that may help diminish the likelihood of bleeding gums and/or the growth of bacteria in your mouth. Also by seeing the dentist while pregnant, you will not need to see one right after the babies are born!

In some cases, gums swollen by pregnancy gingivitis can react strongly to irritants and form large lumps. These growths, called pregnancy tumors, are not cancerous and are generally painless. If the tumor persists, it may require removal by a periodontist. Let your OB-GYN and/or perinatologist know if you feel a lump in your mouth. Sometimes bleeding gums signify a problem with blood clotting. If in addition to bleeding gums you bruise easily, have frequent or heavy nosebleeds or experience bleeding in other parts of your body, let your doctor know.

If you cannot afford dental care, your state may have an assistance program. Contact your state dental society to see if there are programs in your area. You may also want to call a free/low cost medical clinic in your area to ask about dental care. Some dental schools provide lower-cost dental care. Your state dental society can tell you if a dental school clinic is located in your area.

Prenatal Classes

A high-risk pregnancy is less stressful when you know what to expect. Therefore, in addition to reading resources like this book, MOST encourages expectant parents of high-risk twins, and all triplets, quadruplets, quintuplets or more to take advantage of childbirth, high-risk pregnancy, multiple birth, Cesarean section (C-section) and other parent education classes that may be available to them. Some classes may be available privately in your own home. Even parents who have previously taken Lamaze or other childbirth preparation courses may benefit from classes with a specific focus on high-risk pregnancies, multiples, older siblings and C-sections since higher-order multiple pregnancies are likely to be quite different than a singleton pregnancy.

Classes are typically available through the hospital where you plan to deliver, insurance programs, health care provider practices, private sources, and sometimes, local parent resource organizations. Start by asking your health care provider for information about classes he/she recommends. You should also check with your insurance carrier and the hospital where you plan to deliver. Some local parents of multiples support groups might also be able to provide details about local specialty prenatal class resources.

Be sure to look at class options early during your pregnancy to ensure you are still able to attend before becoming too uncomfortable, put on bedrest or possibly hospitalized. If you are home on bedrest, some hospitals will have resources or contacts that can come to your home. If you are hospitalized during your pregnancy, ask to have these classes at bedside before the babies are born, or ask if your physician will allow you to travel to the class in a wheelchair or on a stretcher. If none of these options are available, there may be DVDs or online webinars available you to access from your home or while you are hospitalized.

Preparing for the NICU

Many babies born before 37 weeks gestation will spend some time in the Neonatal Intensive Care Unit (NICU) or the transitional (sometimes called step down) unit. Since almost all higher-order multiple infants are born before 37 weeks, and many twins, most spend at least some time in the NICU. If your babies are born close to 37 weeks they may only spend a day or two longer than you in the hospital.

The length of time your infants will spend in the NICU depends on gestation at delivery, general health and any complications that arise. Infants must be able to maintain body temperature, breathe on their own, and in most cases, feed from a bottle or breast to go home. Weight gain is important, but premature infants are not released from the NICU based on a set weight goal. The following chart shows the average hospital stay based on the MOST Medical Birth survey.

Infant complications largely depend on the delivery gestation. If a mother delivers at 35 weeks, the babies may just need a little time to feed and grow before discharge. However, if delivery occurs between 23-28 weeks, the babies will face significantly more challenges and spend many more days in the NICU.

Babies born prematurely frequently experience some problems coordinating the sucking, swallowing and breathing process which may mean the infant requires a feeding tube for a short time. The coordination of sucking, swallowing and breathing is not expected to be fully developed until about 36 weeks gestational age. This is

MOST Medical Birth Survey: Average Days Infants Were Hospitalized After Birth by Gestation and Type					
Gestation	**Twins**	**Triplets**	**Quadruplets**	**Quintuplets**	**Sextuplets**
24 weeks or less		74.4	69.7		
25 weeks		116.7	90	103.3	
26 weeks		95.9	84.9	138	
27 weeks		84.1	73.3	102.7	
28 weeks		63.6	70.9	104.4	180.4
29 weeks		55.6	68.7	52.3	87.2
30 weeks	48.3	45.2	40.3	50.9	
31 weeks		35.6	37.4	38.6	49.9
32 weeks		26.8	30.5	28.5	52.5
33 weeks		21.1	24.5	19.7	
34 weeks	11	14.4	14.6	20.4	
35 weeks	2.3	9.5	9.36		
36 weeks	3	6.9	8.8	4.3	
37 weeks	3.8	5.5	5		
38 weeks	3.6				

Note: The average gestation for triplets is 33 weeks. Hospital stays for infants born after 35 weeks may vary depending on the size and overall health of the babies.

very normal. Other medical complications of multiple births due to prematurity include jaundice, breathing problems requiring intubation or surfactant treatment for the lungs and blood transfusions. These treatments are all very common and to be expected for babies born preterm. Although less common, more serious complications such as intraventricular hemorrhage (IVH), periventricular leukomalacia (PVL), necrotizing enterocolitis (NEC), retinopathy of prematurity (ROP) and infection do occur especially if delivery occurs before 30 weeks.

Having both parents tour the NICU is a great way to prepare for the delivery of multiples! The best time to take the tour is between 16 and 24 weeks gestation on a day you are scheduled for other testing in the same facility or are in the area. MOST strongly suggests that you use a wheelchair to minimize walking during your tour no matter how strong you feel. Prepare for the tour using the second spiral notebook or an NICU Notebook you have started by creating a list of questions to ask and professionals to meet prior to delivery such as the NICU lactation consultant and the NICU social worker.

For many parents the more they understand about the NICU prior to having their babies in the NICU, the less scary or overwhelming this medical unit is. These types of checklists are already provided in the MOST *NICU Notebook: A Parents Journal* (contact MOST for availability) which also includes a NICU glossary and journaling space among many other things. This book can be exceptionally helpful, but you can use your own notebook as well. MOST also recommends parents review one or more of the resources listed below to become familiar with the terminology, types of professionals and medical equipment they may encounter in the NICU environment.

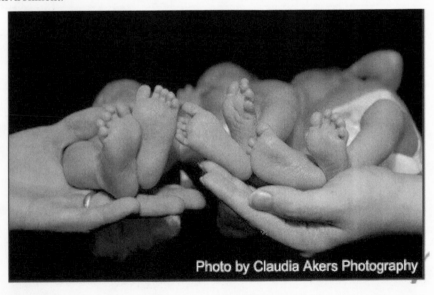

Photo by Claudia Akers Photography

References

(5)   Martin JA, Hamilton BE, Ventura SJ, et al. Births: Final data for 2009.
        National vital statistics reports; vol 60 no 1. Hyattsville, MD: National
        Center for Health Statistics. 2011.
        http://www.cdc.gov/nchs/data/nvsr/nvsr60/nvsr60_01.pdf (accessed
        June 22, 2012).

(6)   Vergnes, J N, and M Sixou. "Preterm Low Birth Weight and Maternal
        Periodontal Status: A Meta-Analysis." *American Journal of Obstetrics
        and Gynecology* 196, no. 2 (2007): 135.

(7)   Conde-Agudelo, A, L Villar, and M Lindheimer. "Maternal Infection and Risk
        of Pre-eclampsia: Systematic Review and Meta-analysis." *American
        Journal of Obstetrics and Gynecology* 198, no. 1 (2008): 7-22.

Resources

Maternal-Fetal Medicine Specialists

- Society for Maternal-Fetal Medicine:
  www.smfm.org/index.cfm?zone=info&nav=about#B

- State Board of Medical Examiners or State Medical Board

- American College of Obstetricians and Gynecologists: www.acog.org

NICU Preparation

- MOST's Infant Multiples package provides additional information about
  NICUs and what a parent needs to know prior to delivery:
  www.MOSTonline.org/sunshop/index.php?l=product_detail&p=74

- For information on premature infants visit PreemieCare:
  www.PreemieCare.org a division of MOST

- Discharge planning info:
  www.MOSTonline.org/preemieBB/viewforum.php?f=69

- Going home parent's checklist: www.MOSTonline.org/preemieBB/viewtopic.php?t=26

- PreemieCare NICU Glossary (PDF) for a list of acronyms and terms related to premature infants: www.PreemieCare.org/Glossary.pdf

- *Your Premature Baby* by Frank Manginello, MD and Theresa Foy DiGeronimo, M.Ed.

Chapter 3: Prenatal Care in a High-risk Twin & Higher-Order Multiple Pregnancy

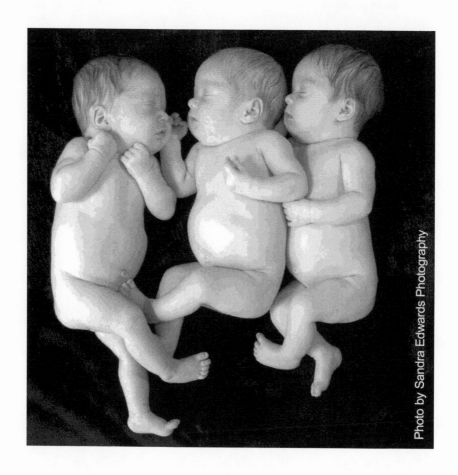

T his chapter covers various aspects of the high-risk and the higher-order multiple pregnancy that differ from a singleton pregnancy. This chapter includes an informational section written by one of the nation's leading authorities on high-risk and higher-order multiple pregnancies, information about feeling your babies' movements while pregnant and nutrition during a multiple pregnancy.

The first section about managing higher-order multiple pregnancies is written by Dr. John Elliott, one of the most experienced higher-order multiple perinatologists in the world. Although written for high order multiples, much of the information is applicable to twin pregnancies. He and his practice have delivered over 800 sets of triplets, over 90 sets of quadruplets and additional quintuplet and sextuplet pregnancies. MOST is grateful for the many years he has supported our organization and the families we support and thankful that he agreed to share his expertise here. As you read his article, keep in mind that you need to speak with your doctor before taking any supplements or medications mentioned.

A Perinatologist's Perspective on Managing Higher-Order Multiple Pregnancies by John Elliott, MD Director of Perinatal Services, Southwest Contemporary Women's Care, Mesa AZ

The human female is most successful when carrying only one baby during pregnancy. Multiple gestation not only increases the risks of a less than perfect outcome, but in general, means the mother cannot continue her normal lifestyle. In order to improve her chances of a good outcome, the mother must alter her daily patterns of activity, diet and lifestyle. Each additional baby in the uterus literally almost doubles the pregnancy risk (i.e., triplets are twice the risk of twins, and quadruplets are twice the risk of triplets).

Newer infertility technologies have solved many couples' relentless and frantic struggle to have a baby; however, these technologies have also created a higher incidence of multiple gestations including a 3 to 4% incidence of triplets and a 1% incidence of quadruplets with Pergonal or

GIFT procedures. These families then face difficult decisions when they learn of their "good fortune." The physicians from whom they seek advice often recommend embryo reduction to twins or a singleton, which is an unacceptable option for many of these couples. What can be done to try to give this family the best possible chance at a good outcome while carrying a triplet or a quadruplet pregnancy?

Over the past 30 years, I have gained a tremendous amount of hands-on experience providing care to higher-order multiple gestations. Since our first quadruplet pregnancy in 1984, we have delivered 2 sets of sextuplets, 12 sets of quintuplets, 100+ sets of quadruplets and more than 800 sets of triplets. About half of the quadruplet and more than 10% of the triplet pregnancies have come from other states and countries. Our outcomes have been published (references 8-11) which confirm that our approach to managing higher-order multiple gestations is successful most of the time. Based on this experience, we have published over 20 medical articles and book chapters on the management of multiple gestation pregnancies. Here is our approach written in layman terms.

The most important thing that you as an expectant mother of triplets, quadruplets, or more can do is realize the seriousness of the situation. It is almost 100% certain that you will have a premature delivery, as the average gestational age at delivery for triples is approximately 33 weeks and for quadruplets it is approximately 29-32 weeks (a full-term singleton delivery is 40 weeks). [Note: MOST families tend to do a little better.] Your goal is to beat the average and go as long as possible with your higher-order multiple pregnancy.

First Trimester (0-13 Weeks)

For some expectant mothers, the first 13 weeks are spent in survival mode. Ovarian hyperstimulation and hyperemesis gravidarum (severe morning sickness) are not uncommon and can produce symptoms than can be debilitating. Standard measures to reduce nausea and vomiting include: small feedings of bland foods, fresh ginger, acupuncture or acupressure, hypnosis and antinausea medications (Phenergan, Compazine, Tigan, Reglan or Zofran). Work with your OB-GYN or Perinatologist. If all methods fail, steroids will work in about 80% of resistant cases. We start with IV dexamethasone then switch to oral prednisone tapering to the lowest effective dose and then stopping after 2-3 weeks. We try to avoid placement of a central IV line (PICC line) as these have a greater than 50% complication rate in pregnancy. (12)

When tolerating food, aggressive weight gain is the goal for the rest of the pregnancy. We recommend 3500-4000 calories per day with a high protein intake (>1.5 gm/kg of body weight). Barbara Luke's book *When You Are Expecting Twins, Triplets or Quads* is excellent and should be the "bible" for nutrition and supplements in a higher-order multiple pregnancy. Your goal is a weight gain of 50-75 pounds with triplets and 75-100 pounds with quadruplets or more.

Testing and Supplements

If desired, a special ultrasound can be done at 11-14 weeks to measure the NT (nuchal thickness) of the babies' necks. If excessively thick, this may be an indication of increased risk of Down Syndrome in that baby. Chorionic villus sampling (CVS) may be done to "biopsy" the placenta (11-13 weeks) to determine if the baby does have Down Syndrome or an amniocentesis can be performed at 15-18 weeks. There is also a blood test available where fetal DNA is recovered from the mother's blood which can determine if all the babies do not have Down Syndrome or if one or more do have Down Syndrome, but it will not identify which baby is affected. [Note: CVS and amniocentesis are invasive procedures with a risk of infection and miscarriage. You should have an idea if this will change your decision to continue the pregnancy.] We recommend one baby aspirin (81 mg) and extra calcium (2000 mg) (4 Tums) starting before 15 weeks.

Second Trimester (13-24 weeks)

The course of your pregnancy is largely influenced by the number of living babies you are carrying. If you started with quadruplets, but had a spontaneous loss of 1 fetus, you would be expected to have the same risks of a triplet pregnancy. As noted in Table 1 below, the average age at delivery for multiple gestations is:

Table 1: Average Gestation at Delivery	
Singleton	40 weeks
Twins (without reduction)	36.5 weeks
Twins (following a reduction)	35.5 weeks
Triplets	33 weeks
Quadruplets	29.5 weeks
Quintuplets	28 weeks
Note: Gestational averages in this table were obtained from a variety of medical studies and literature and may be slightly different from the CDC averages listed in Chapter 1 of this book. This data has been included to provide additional information not available from the CDC such as the gestational average after a fetal reduction.	

An ultrasound should be done at 20 weeks to examine the anatomy of your babies to determine any identifiable malformations. It is also very important to know how many placentas there are. Sometimes one of your embryos will split after implantation in your uterus resulting in identical twins that may share a placenta. This can be dangerous if a rare complication called Twin-to-Twin Transfusion Syndrome (TTTS) develops. It is ideal if there is one placenta for each fetus. TTTS is extremely rare and only occurs in approximately 10% of all monochorionic pregnancies in the United States, which amounts to about 2,000 pregnancies per year. (13)

At 16 weeks, a vaginal ultrasound should measure the length of the cervix (CL ultrasound). This CL measurement should be repeated every 1 to 2 weeks until 26 weeks to assess for a possible incompetent cervix that occurs in only about 5% of twins and 10% of higher order multiple gestations. If the cervical length is less than 2 cm, strong consideration should be given to placing a cervical cerclage (stitch) to support the weakened cervical tissue. Growth ultrasound scans should be done every 3-4 weeks.

Preterm labor occurs early in higher-order multiple gestation (22 weeks average in our quadruplets), so we strongly recommend the use of a home contraction monitor starting at 18 weeks gestation in quadruplet and 20 weeks in triplet pregnancies. [If you call the MOST office between 16-18 weeks, they can teach you how to monitor yourself for contractions so that you can begin to get in tune with the changes in your body prior to needing the home monitor.] The gestational age is very important because the highest rate of loss in quadruplet pregnancies is between 19 and 22 weeks. Loss of the pregnancy at this gestational age is not well known by physicians and patients, so physicians should be made aware of this. We watch the number of contractions the mother is having. (Note that you probably will not feel many of these contractions, but the monitor picks them up.) We average the number of contractions per hour over a one week period of time (14 individual contraction counts) to give us the average number of contractions for that week. (14)

When the average number of contractions is about 3.5 per hour or higher, we strongly consider the use of tocolytic drugs (medications that will stop contractions). Choices of oral medications to reduce contractions include Nifedipine (dose 10 mg to 20 mg every 4-6 hours) or ibuprofen (600 g every 6 hours). We attempt to keep patients at home as long as possible because they are more comfortable, will eat better, and have the constant support of their families there, which they would not have in the hospital. Hospitalization is reserved for complications.

Weekly pelvic examinations are also done to check for any change of your cervix and to assess whether the lowest baby is starting to push its head or rear end into your pelvis. Contractions generally are not harmful until the lowest baby's presenting part is down against the cervix. Small, frequent contractions can cause your cervix to thin and dilate. If you do go into preterm labor, you need to be aware that you may be treated with medications such as magnesium sulfate, which have some significant side effects. These medications are necessary to try to stop the preterm labor and may have to be used in very high doses, which may make you feel very weak and drained and could cause double and/or blurred vision. You and your physician should be aware that the preterm labor during a higher-order multiple pregnancy may not stop as easily as with a singleton patient in preterm labor. It often takes 3 to 4 days to stop preterm labor in triplets or quadruplets and the effort should continue despite the mother's discomfort. At this point, your psychological strength will be called upon to get you through a very uncomfortable situation. You must be able to disregard your own physical discomfort in order to get through this episode and give your babies more time. (13)

Another dilemma involves the use of steroids to help mature the babies' lungs if delivery is threatened. In some patients with triplets or quadruplets, the steroids will increase and intensify the contractions of your uterus so preterm labor may worsen because of the medication being given to help the babies breathe if preterm labor cannot be stopped. This medical fact is not well known by physicians, and we only learned it the hard way with several of our quadruplet mothers.

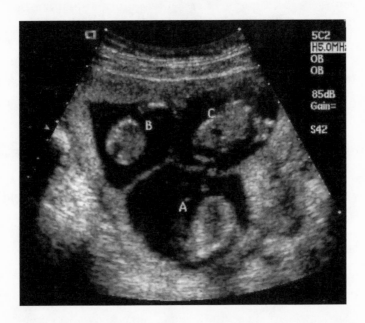

Patients need to be aware that many OB-GYN physicians and perinatologists believe that tocolytic drugs (magnesium sulfate, Terbutaline, Indocin, Nifedipine) only work for a short time (48 hours), so they will not use these medications aggressively involving high doses for a prolonged period of time (weeks or months). This is potentially very dangerous to your pregnancy as preterm labor that starts again after treatment with tocolytics may lead to a very early delivery. **This situation can almost always be prevented by aggressive use of tocolytic drugs.** If delivery is going to occur at less than 32 weeks, your doctor should give you magnesium sulfate prior to the delivery. It would be ideal for 12 hours, but any magnesium before delivery may be helpful. There is evidence that magnesium reduces the chance that your babies will develop cerebral palsy (a severe neurologic handicap).

On a final note, while progesterone (17P) therapy has been used successfully to decrease the risk of preterm delivery (PTD) in singletons with a history of preterm delivery (PTD) in a prior pregnancy, progesterone has not been successful in decreasing PTD in twins and at this time should NOT be used in higher-order multiple gestations.

Third Trimester (24-36 weeks)

Preeclampsia (aka toxemia) is a medical complication of triplet and quadruplet pregnancies and was the reason for delivery in many of our quadruplet pregnancies. If you develop preeclampsia despite the baby aspirin therapy, it is important that your doctors watch the babies' health very carefully by biophysical profile monitoring with the ultrasound machine. Depending on the severity of your condition, this special ultrasound can be done twice a week or even every day in more severe cases.

In addition, to recommending MOST to all of our expectant parents of multiples, we suggest finding a local support group for women on bed rest. There are many fine support groups throughout the country that participate in high-risk pregnancies. We feel that support parents are very important to the team because they have been through most of the physical, emotional, and psychological challenges that you are experiencing. Nothing beats firsthand experience and some of the things that they learned in dealing and coping with these stresses can be passed on to you, which makes our job as physicians much easier. I often call on our triplet and quadruplet mothers when I need a cheerleader to get an expectant mother through a particularly rocky time. I am deeply indebted to these very dedicated, giving people. The mothers of multiples are very close to each other because of the friendships developed during each of their individual struggles. If all goes well, our goal is to deliver quadruplets, quintuplets, and sextuplets at 34 weeks and triplets at 35 weeks because this gestational age will give the best result for both the mother and the babies.

Well, does it work? As I mentioned earlier, there is no substitute for experience, and that includes the doctor. We have learned an incredible amount from each of our patients and are able to apply that information to the next expectant mother of triplets or more who faces the daunting task of trying to get through pregnancy with 3 or more healthy babies and to minimize the risks of prematurity. Our 2 sextuplet pregnancies delivered at 29-1/2 weeks and 30-5/7 weeks with 4 healthy babies (2 stillbirths) and 6 healthy babies, respectively. Our 12 quintuplet pregnancies delivered at 32-1/2 weeks average gestational age (the national average is 28 weeks) and 58 babies are healthy. There were two deaths (one with a significant heart abnormality). Our quadruplets delivered at 32-1/7 weeks average gestational age with the national average being 29-1/2 weeks. There have been 8 neonatal deaths and ~3% incidence of major handicaps in our surviving quad babies.

I do not want to lead you to believe that these pregnancies do not involve significant risks because if a mother delivers at 26 or 27 weeks, she would have 3 or 4 babies at risk of dying or living with the possibility of permanent handicaps. What I do want to offer you as parents facing the choice between a reduction and carrying 3 or 4 babies is some reasonable medical experience that will support a decision to carry your pregnancy if you understand the risk of prematurity. For more information, please contact me at johnelliott65@yahoo.com.

MOST greatly appreciates Dr. Elliott for writing the above section.

Different physicians may use other approaches and techniques to manage a higher-order multiple birth. Dr. Elliott has had so much success with his protocol that we are providing below a bibliography of articles published on his results for expectant families to use or share with their physicians.

- Elliott, JP. "Preterm Labor in Twins and High-order Multiples." *Clinics in Perinatology* 5, No. 34 (2005):599-604.

- Elliott, JP, Istwan NB, Collins A, et al. "Indicated and Nonindicated Preterm Delivery in Twin Gestations: Impact on Neonatal Outcome and Cost." *Journal of Perinatology* 25 (2004):4-7.

- Elliott, JP. "Management of High-Order Multiple Gestation." *Clinics in Perinatology* 32, No. 2 (2005):387-402.

- Elliott JP, Flynn M, Kaemmerer EL, et al. "Terbutaline Pump Tocolysis in High Order Multiples." *The Journal of Reproductive Medicine* 42 (1997):687-693.

- Elliott JP, Radin TG. "Serum Magnesium Levels During Magnesium Sulfate Tocolysis in High Order Multiple Gestations." *The Journal of Reproductive Medicine* 40 (1995):45.

- Elliott JP, Istwan NB, Rhea D, et al. "The Occurrence of Adverse Events in Women Receiving Continuous Subcutaneous Terbutaline Therapy." *American Journal of Obstetrics and Gynecology* 19, No. 1 (2004):1277-1282.

- Elliott JP. "Preterm Labor." *Clinics in Perinatology* 34, No. 4 (December 2007):599-609, vii.

- Elliott JP, Istwan NB, Rhea DJ, Desch CN, Stanziano GJ. "The Impact on Acute Tocolysis on Neonatal Outcome in Women Hospitalized with Preterm Labor at 32 to 34 Weeks Gestation." *American Journal of Perinatology* 26, No. 2 (February 2009):123-128.

- Elliott JP, Lewis DF, Morrison JC, Garite TJ. "In Defense of Magnesium Sulfate." *Obstetrics & Gynecology* 113, No. 6 (June 2009):1341-1348.

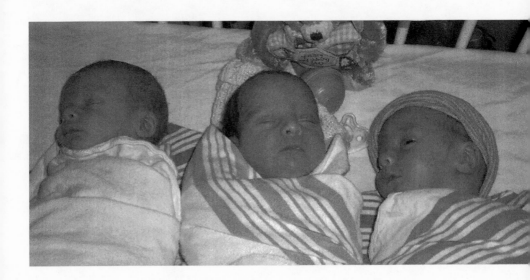

Weight Gain and Nutrition: Goals and Expectations

Why Nutrition is So Important

Good nutrition helps babies achieve higher birth weights and assures optimal prenatal development of the babies' teeth. When a baby is born, all 20 primary teeth and some permanent teeth are in various stages of formation. Babies DO NOT absorb calcium from the mother's teeth during pregnancy. This is a myth. Premature babies who have been properly nourished in the womb have fewer illnesses and recover from them more quickly. Proper nutrition during pregnancy helps the mother recover quicker and with fewer long-term effects that could result from prolonged bedrest and the extra weight gain needed for a multiple pregnancy.

You may qualify for a national food program called WIC (Women, Infants, Children) while pregnant. WIC can provide supplemental foods, health care referrals and nutrition education for low-income pregnant, breastfeeding and non-breastfeeding postpartum women, as well as to infants and children up to age 5 who are found to be at nutritional risk. [See resources at the end of this chapter or check your local phone book for your state office.] Your doctor's office may also be able to help you. Do not feel embarrassed to use these sources to obtain healthy food for your babies.

What is the Optimal Weight Gain?

In determining the optimal weight gain, medical professionals must consider pre-pregnancy weight to adjust the ideal amount of weight gain for each pregnancy. Early pregnancy weight gain and steady weight gain are the most important, and in higher-order multiple pregnancies, many professionals recommend these guidelines for early weight gain:

- Twin pregnancy: 24 pounds gained by 24 weeks gestation
- Triplet pregnancy: 36 pounds gained by 24 weeks gestation
- Quadruplet pregnancy: 50 pounds gained by 24 weeks gestation [15]

If you are able to achieve this goal you are on your way toward your ultimate goal for the whole pregnancy (see list below). If you are not, some things can be adjusted such as the types of food eaten, supplements taken, etc. The goals above are ideal weight gains and what you should aim for; however, you may not be able to gain this much. You also might not need to gain this much if you were significantly overweight when you began your pregnancy, but you might need to gain more if you were underweight. If you lost some weight at the beginning of your pregnancy, you can count any weight gain from your lowest weight toward your goal! Please do not feel like a failure or give up because you see this goal as unattainable.

Recommended weight gain may not always be possible due to hyperemesis (severe morning sickness) and your physician may make different recommendations, but ideally the early weight loss or slow weight gain in early pregnancy should be made up by 24 weeks gestation. In addition, the number of babies involved in the pregnancy will affect the expected weight gain. The total weight gain range for each type of pregnancy is listed below:

- Twin pregnancy: 40-50 pounds

- Triplet pregnancy: 50-60 pounds
- For a quad pregnancy: 65-80 pounds [15]

A woman who begins her multiple gestation pregnancy overweight may safely gain 10 pounds less than recommended. This is probably the only time in your life when being heavier than you want to be is actually a good thing! Some mothers have a difficult time gaining weight. Sometimes the difficulty is a result of:

- Constipation (See tips for avoiding later in this section)

- Nausea or "morning" sickness (See chapter 4 for more information and suggestions to reduce nausea)

- Not eating frequently (Try to eat smaller amounts every hour or two)

- Too much activity (Burning too many calories with your activity rather than the calories going to the babies)

- Heartburn or indigestion

-

How To Enhance Optimal Weight Gain

Try to gain weight early in your pregnancy as many mothers find they are not able to eat as much later due to the decreased space for the stomach as the babies grow and some of the medications needed to prolong the pregnancy decrease the appetite. Also, remember that your pregnancy will not last a full 40 weeks.

1. Relax; anxiety can lead to decreased appetite (and worry lines on your forehead!)

2. Make sure you eat healthy foods including balanced portions of proteins, carbohydrates and fats.

3. Schedule visitors at mealtimes for company.

4. You should choose foods that give the most nutrition for the calories, such as milk, hard-boiled eggs, peanuts (if you do not have an allergy), milkshakes and yogurt.

5. Keeping a food diary helps identify when and what foods can be added to increase daily caloric intake.

6. Fluids should be taken between meals to allow room for food during meal.

7. Try to avoid nausea and constipation.

8. Additional tricks to eating more than you have ever before include cutting your sandwiches in quarters and use bread instead of a roll.

9. Increase the amount of meat in your sandwich. Eat all the time. Graze throughout the day.

10. Ask your doctor for a consultation with a nutritionist or someone familiar with weight gaining strategies during pregnancy.

11. Eat ice cream!

How To Avoid or Decrease Constipation

1. Remember to drink plenty of fluids especially water and fruit juices

2. Eat high fiber grains such as bran and wheat germ

3. Eat more raw fruits and vegetables

4. Eat at regular times

5. Drink hot water with 1 teaspoon lemon juice 3 times a day

6. Ask your physician for a stool softener (do not take any over the counter medications without asking physician as some may interfere with other medications and supplements)

7. With your doctor's permission spread out the supplements and vitamins you are taking throughout the day. Taking all of them or several of them at the same time can be tough on your stomach and can lead to constipation (and/or nausea)

These measures are important because your decreased activity level may lead to constipation and constipation may lead to decreased appetite. Therefore, it is important to decrease or eliminate constipation. Consult a nutritionist or dietician if needed. Your insurance may cover this type of care if you have a physician's referral. Some OB-GYN offices have nutritionists who work with their patients.

The suggested caloric requirement for a triplet pregnancy is 4,000 calories a day. By comparison, the average caloric requirement for a non-pregnant woman is 2,200 calories a day, so you need to try to eat much more. Calories are your friend! Calories should be divided as listed below:

- 20% from Protein (about 800 calories)
- 40% from Carbohydrates (about 1600 calories)
- 40% from Fats (about 1600 calories)

How To Minimize Heartburn and Indigestion

It is not uncommon for indigestion and heartburn to start about 22 weeks but for most it does not start until 26-28 weeks depending upon how many babies you are carrying. Here are a few tips that may help. Get some inexpensive vanilla ice cream (NOT high quality). Eat a teaspoon before every bite of whatever you are eating whether at breakfast, dinner, snack, regardless of the time of day. This will help to coat your esophagus. Try not to lie down for at least a ½ hour after eating. Lay in a recliner or sit propped up in bed before lying down for a nap. Try to identify if certain food or drink is causing this discomfort. It could be something as common as water and if that is the case drink juice instead. It could also be the typical culprits such as gravies or sauces. Listen to your body and try eliminating these items.

Planning Your Calorie Intake

We are including some recommendations on foods to eat and the number of servings to eat below. The elements of a balanced diet include protein, complex carbohydrates, fats, fruits and vegetables. You can also consult the government website, http://www.choosemyplate.gov/, for examples of daily serving sizes of many foods. Note that some food are listed under more than one category and can be counted for all the categories. For example, whole milk can count as a protein serving, a fat serving and your liquid intake.

- **Proteins (meats, seafood, poultry, dairy products)** - Proteins are the body's basic building blocks. Extra protein is needed to build the placentas to allow for increases in breast, uterine tissue and blood volume and to promote the babies' growth. Red meats are rich in iron and pregnant mothers should have two 3oz. servings a day. Eggs, peanut butter and fish are also good sources of protein. Some fish (such as shark, swordfish, king mackerel, tuna and tilefish) may contain too much mercury and should be avoided. The FDA says to limit intake of fish considered lower in mercury to 2 meals per week (6 oz serving each). These fish include shrimp, salmon, pollock and catfish. Check with local advisories to determine the safety of fish caught locally by family and friends. Milk and dairy products should be the full fat versions. Cottage cheese, milk, yogurt and cheese provide protein. Expectant mothers of triplets should consume 10 daily servings of protein. Expectant mothers of quadruplets should consume 12 daily servings of protein.

- **Carbohydrates (breads, cereals, pasta, fruits)** - Carbohydrates provide the energy needed for both mother and babies. Fiber is a non-digestible form of carbohydrate, which is important to avoid constipation. Carbohydrates also help to maintain regular blood-sugar level. Whole grains, a common and inexpensive source of carbohydrates, are rich in fiber, B vitamins and are often fortified with other vitamins. Complex carbohydrates, like whole grains, are better than simple carbohydrates like sugar. Expectant mothers of triplets and quadruplets should consume 12 daily servings of carbohydrates a day: preferably whole grain.

- **Fats (dairy products, nuts and oils)** - Fats promote proper nerve development, and fat-soluble vitamins A and D are important for nerve development and tissue growth. Dairy is a source of fat and the richest source of calcium. Calcium is needed to build babies' bones and teeth. While mothers do not lose calcium from their teeth during pregnancy, the babies will take calcium stores from the mother's body if her diet does not provide enough. Dairy is also a good source of protein. Dairy foods are particularly good to eat at night because they are slowly digested and help decrease nighttime hunger. Mothers should NOT take prenatal vitamins with milk since the calcium competes with the iron for absorption. Expectant mothers of triplets should consume 10 dairy and 7 other fat servings per day. Expectant mothers of quadruplets should consume 12 dairy and 8 other fat servings per day.

- **Fruits and Vegetables** - Fruits and vegetables are a great source of fiber, have high water content and provide good sources of folic acid and vitamins A and C. Taking prenatal vitamins with orange or grapefruit juice helps absorb the iron. With fruits and vegetables the deeper the color, the more nutritious the food; however, the mother should not fill up on salads at the expense of the meats. Someone following a vegetarian diet may have difficulty consuming all the required nutrients and should consult a dietitian for a multiple pregnancy. Expectant mothers of triplets should consume 4 vitamin C rich (strawberries, lemons, oranges, kiwi, grapefruit, peaches, kale, peppers, Brussels sprouts, etc.), 4 vitamin A rich foods (liver, butter/margarine, hard cheese, carrots, sweet potatoes, spinach, mangoes, apricots, etc.) and 5 other fruit/vegetable servings per day. Expectant mothers of quadruplets should consume 4 vitamin C rich foods, 4 vitamin A rich foods and 6 other fruit/vegetable servings per day

- **Nutritional Supplements** - Supplements are specially formulated foods, usually in beverage form, containing extra calories and/or protein. If you want to take nutritional supplements, you should tell your physician. Many pregnant mothers do take these and your doctor may have some specific recommendations. Supplements are available in three types:

- Basic supplements – Boost, Ensure and Carnation Instant Breakfast

- High-calorie or high-protein supplements – the "plus" varieties of regular supplements

- High-calorie and high-protein supplements – not as readily available but may be ordered from a specialty merchant. (Often these supplements are sweet and can trigger nausea, appetite depression and diarrhea.)

- **Vitamins, Herbs and Medications** - As with nutritional supplements you need to speak with your physician in advance about any vitamins or herbs you might take because some have adverse effects or may counteract or interfere with the supplements and medications your doctor has already recommended for you. You should not take any prescription medicine, over-the-counter medicines or "home remedies," without checking with the doctor to assure safety in pregnancy. It is not uncommon to hear that even the prescribed prenatal vitamins cannot be tolerated by mothers, so tell your doctor if you have that problem. The following are some minerals commonly advised by physicians:

Calcium – Calcium can reduce high blood pressure and the occurrence of preterm labor. In addition, it can relieve heartburn. Adequate intake is very important to prevent osteoporosis in the future as well. Calcium should be started at about 15 weeks.

Magnesium – Magnesium keeps the uterus from contracting, is helpful against heartburn and may protect the babies' developing nervous systems.

Zinc – Zinc is vital for the development of babies' nervous systems, lowers the chance of infection and can prevent the premature rupture of membranes by blocking the formation of hormones that can trigger premature labor. Cod liver or other fish oil provides a good source of zinc. Zinc is recommended for pregnant women with a history of preeclampsia or hypertension and is available in a gel cap form. It may cause loose stools until the body adjusts. Look for the "burp-free" kind.

- **Water and Other Liquids** - Liquid intake is extremely important for a variety of reasons. Your blood supply is rapidly increasing as the placentas and babies grow. You can easily become dehydrated and may not realize you are dehydrated until you have problems. You do not want to find out you are dehydrated by going to the emergency room with contractions! Drinking enough water helps:

  ○ Prevent dehydration which can trigger uterine contractions
  ○ Protect against urinary tract infections (UTI) caused by hormonal changes
  ○ Maintains normal body temperature despite an increased metabolism
  ○ Relieve constipation caused by hormonal changes
  ○ Reduce headaches, dry skin and complexion problems

The goal for mothers expecting triplets or more is to consume 1 gallon of liquid per day. That is equivalent to 8 glasses with 2 cups (16 oz) of liquid in each. One way to achieve that goal is to keep water within reach at all times. You can also fill two ½ gallon containers with water every morning and try to finish both by the end of the day. Another trick many mothers have found helpful is to flavor the water with a little lemon. The taste is appealing and the lemon will make you thirsty: a win/win for hydration. If you are in a warm and/or dry environment, additional water is needed. Lemon can also help decrease constipation and gas. Milk, juice and soup all count as liquids but limit coffee and other caffeinated drinks to 1 or 2 cups per day. You may want to eliminate all caffeine as it can act as a diuretic and may even irritate your bladder. You will know when you are drinking enough fluids because you will urinate regularly and your urine will be pale in color.

Important Note: As with any pregnancy avoid alcohol and cigarettes, even second hand smoke. Basic pregnancy books can provide more details of what you cannot eat during pregnancy and nutritious foods to enjoy.

Photo by Claudia Akers Photography

References

(8)   Francois, K, C Sears, R Wilson, M Foley, and J P Elliott. "Neonatal Outcome of Quadruplet Pregnancies: Twelve Year Experience at a Single Institution." In *21st Annual Society for Maternal-Fetal Medicine Conference, February 5-10*. Reno, Nevada: Society for Maternal-Fetal Medicine, 2001.

(9)   Francois, K, C Sears, R Wilson, M Foley, and J P Elliott. "Maternal Morbidity and Obstetrical Complications of Quadruplet Pregnancy: Twelve-Year Experience at a Single Institution." In *21st Annual Society for Maternal-Fetal Medicine Conference, February 5-10*. Reno, Nevada: Society for Maternal-Fetal Medicine, 2001.

(10)   Francois, K, C Sears, R Wilson, M Foley, and L P Elliott. "Twelve-Year Experience of Quadruplet Pregnancies at a Single Institution." In *21st Annual Society for Maternal-Fetal Medicine Conference, February 5-10*. Reno, Nevada: Society for Maternal-Fetal Medicine, 2001.

(11)   Francois, K, C Sears, R Wilson, M Foley, and J P Elliott. "Preterm Labor Complicating Quadruplet Pregnancy: Twelve-Year Experience at a Single Institution." In *21st Annual Society for Maternal-Fetal Medicine Conference, February 5-10*. Reno, Nevada: Society for Maternal-Fetal Medicine Conference, 2001.

(12)   Ogura, J M, K E Francois, J H Perlow, and J P Elliott. "Morbidity Associated with Peripherally Inserted Central Catheter (PICC) Use during Pregnancy." *American Journal of Obstetrics and Gynecology* 188, no. 5 (2003): 1223-1225.

(13)   Quintero, R A, C Comas, P W Bornick, and et al. "Selective versus Non-selective Laser Photocoagulation of Placental Vessels in Twin-to-Twin Transfusion Syndrome." *Ultrasound in Obstetrics & Gynecology* 16 (2000): 230-236.

(14) Elliott, J P. "Management of High-Order Multiple Gestation." *Clinics in Perinatology* 32, no. 2 (2005): 387-402.

(15) Luke, B, and T Eberlein. *When You're Expecting Twins, Triplets, or Quads: Proven Guidelines for a Healthy Multiple Pregnancy*. Revised ed. New York: Harper Collins, 1999.

Resources

Pregnancy Weight Gain

www.healthchecksystems.com/heightweightchart.htm provides guidelines for establishing pre-pregnancy weight and frame size.

Medications during Pregnancy

Mother Risk has information about the safety or risk of drugs, chemicals and disease during pregnancy and lactation at www.motherisk.org/prof/index.jsp

Women's Health

US government site that provides much information about many topics including Pregnancy Do's and Don'ts and Pregnancy Food Don'ts. www.womenshealth.gov/pregnancy/mom-to-be-tools

Chapter 4: Possible Challenges and Treatments during Pregnancy

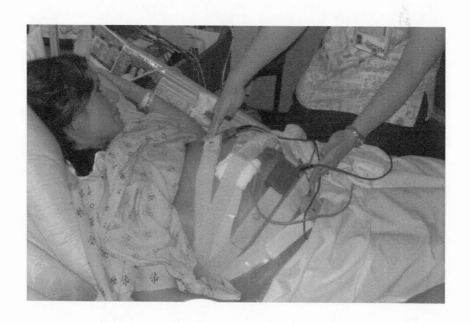

"I made it through a cracked rib, mild preeclampsia and Bell's Palsy. I got Bell's Palsy two days before I delivered. Has this happened to anyone else? With all this said I would like to add that without question it was all worth it. I delivered two girls and a boy at 33.5 weeks."

As with any pregnancy complications can occur. Discuss with your doctor in more detail what you can do to help prevent possible problems or reduce the severity. Below we have listed, in approximate chronological order of appearance during the pregnancy, some challenges or complications that may arise. Please review them thoroughly so you will be familiar with some basic information if, by chance, they happen to you.

Morning Sickness and Hyperemesis

"The reason for my fever is that one of my sites for my Zofran pump got infected. My husband is picking up antibiotics for that now. I will also be put back on the central IV line on Monday. The doctor seemed very disappointed and upset that I fell through the cracks, as I am now a mere 4 pounds away from admission to the hospital and being put on TPN (total nutrition in an IV). The way I have been losing weight lately, I can lose 4 pounds in as little as two days, so it has gotten pretty serious pretty fast. Hopefully the central IV line will come in the nick of time and save me from a hospital stay."

Hyperemesis is a severe form of morning sickness. Many mothers pregnant with a single baby have "morning sickness." However, mothers of multiples are at a higher risk of developing hyperemesis. Some lucky mothers never have morning sickness! Nevertheless, chances are you will have some morning sickness.

Hyperemesis typically occurs during the first and early second trimesters, but for a few mothers, it can last the entire pregnancy. Most expectant mothers experience more nausea on an empty stomach, which is why it commonly occurs in the morning. With severe hyperemesis, the nausea can occur at all times of the day. Women who experience hyper-stimulation of the ovaries may also experience hyperemesis.

Tips for Managing Hyperemesis

- Get out of bed slowly

- Set the room to a much cooler temperature

- Get some fresh air outside

- Take vitamins at the time of day when the nausea is least problematic which for many women is at bedtime or an hour or so after dinner. Sometimes you may need to spread out your supplements and medications throughout the day to make it easier on your stomach. Ask your doctor prior to doing so since some medications may need to be taken at certain times or in combination with other medications or supplements you are taking.

- Avoid stress (or at least try!)

- Avoid brushing your teeth right after eating. Gel toothpaste may be better than a paste.

- Consider using motion sickness wristbands, acupressure, reiki therapy or acupuncture if allowed by your health care professional

- Eat small meals and avoid greasy, spicy or fatty foods. Keep a food log noting what did or did not agree with you and refer to this for future meals.

- Eat a small amount of plain crackers, drink ginger ale or sip crushed ice. Keep them at your bedside and have a little a few minutes before getting up and again before going back to bed if you get up during the night to go to the bathroom.

- Try smelling citrus fruit like lemons, limes or oranges. Some mothers find those odors helpful. Others find that chewing gum helps.

- Avoid sights, smells and sounds that trigger nausea

- Try using fresh ginger to help decrease nausea.

Some mothers find that even the scent of their partner causes nausea. You may want to change his pillowcase every day and ask that he not wear aftershave or cologne if that bothers you.

Treating Hyperemesis

Your doctor may prescribe medication like promethazine (Phenergan), prochlorperazine (Compazine), trimethobenzamide (Tigan), metoclopramide (Reglan) or ondansetron (Zofran) if hyperemesis prevents adequate weight gain or leads to dehydration. Medications can be taken orally, rectally, by injection, via an IV or subcutaneously (under the skin). If dehydration is severe enough you may need IV fluids, IV nutrition and/or hospitalization.

Infections

Certain types of infections can happen during any pregnancy. All require a diagnosis by a doctor and usually antibiotics many of which are safe to use during pregnancy. Ask your doctor what you should look for and when it would be appropriate for you to call or come in.

Urinary Tract Infections (UTI)

UTIs are very common during any pregnancy due to hormonal changes and can trigger premature labor. Symptoms of a UTI include frequent urination, backache, voiding small amounts of urine at a time, painful urination and fever. Treatment for a UTI may require antibiotics and drinking plenty of water.

Yeast Infections

Yeast infections are also common for any expectant mother and mothers expecting higher-order multiples are no exception. Symptoms include:

- Itchiness, irritation, soreness, burning and redness in your vagina and labia (and sometimes swelling)
- An odorless vaginal discharge that is often white, creamy or cottage cheese-like. [*See note.] The discharge may be greenish or have a fishy odor.
- Discomfort or pain during sex (if you are not restricted from having intercourse)
- Burning when you urinate (the urine irritates the skin)

*Note: Do not self treat, even if you have had a yeast infection before. Having a milky white vaginal discharge starting about 16-20 weeks into the pregnancy is not uncommon, but be sure to mention this to your health care provider so infection can be ruled out. Once you are approximately 16 weeks along, we suggest wearing a mini-pad and changing it frequently throughout the day. If you ever go to the hospital with a vaginal discharge (clear fluid, blood red, pink or brown) take your soiled underwear or pad with you in a sealable plastic bag as this may provide important information to your health care provider.

Vaginal Bacterial Infections

Vaginal bacterial infections can also occur during pregnancy. These can cause preterm labor and delivery, so testing for these is important. You will usually be tested between 16 and 20 weeks. If after 22 weeks you do not have this type of infection, you probably will not get one, but if you do get this infection before 20 weeks, it will need to be treated since it can increase your chance of preterm labor. Although these infections can cause increased discharge, fever or an odorous discharge, sometimes mothers have no symptoms.

The two main types of bacterial infections of the vagina you will be tested for are Bacterial Vaginosis (BV) that is a mixed bacteria infection, and Group B strep (GBS). Both of these infections can trigger premature labor, preterm premature rupture of membranes (PPROM) or infection to the amniotic sac, fetus or postpartum incision. They can be treated with prescription antibiotics. In addition, Group B Strep (GBS) can cause a serious infection in the babies that can lead to sepsis, pneumonia, meningitis, neurological damage and in rare cases, even death. Group B Strep is different from the bacteria that cause strep throat: Group A Strep. However, if you have strep throat you need to tell your doctor. In a singleton, non-high-risk pregnancy an expectant mother is generally not tested for Group B strep until much later in her pregnancy, but in a higher-order multiple pregnancy, testing is recommended prior to 20 weeks and always before a cerclage due to the risk of infection with this procedure. To test for these infections a vaginal swab is collected, and if the results are positive, testing will be done again after treatment with antibiotics.

Fifth Disease

Fifth disease (Parvo virus) is a common childhood disease that frequently causes outbreaks in schools. The name was given because it was the fifth rash-causing disease to be described by doctors (the others being scarlet fever, measles, rubella and roseola). Fifth disease causes only mild symptoms in children (low fever, cold symptoms and a "slapped-cheek" rash) and is from a form of the human parvovirus (not the same virus that infects dogs). Fifth disease can lead to potentially fatal anemia and heart problems in a fetus, and the risk of losing the pregnancy completely is 2-9% in infected mothers. A pregnant mother who is exposed to this virus should contact her physician about being tested. Unfortunately, there is no vaccine available at this time. You may want to try to stay away from small children or limit your exposure to them, especially when they are ill. While pregnant you should try to avoid catching whatever is going around as much as possible: any virus, cold, flu, disease or infection. If you have young children, especially toddlers and preschoolers, make sure they wash their hands when they come home. You also may want to use an alcohol based hand wipe to clean their hands when they get in the car.

Anemia

"My OB-GYN told me to take extra iron and extra folic acid (2mg extra for triplets). Per my doctor's suggestion, I always take my 2 iron pills with an orange or orange juice and take them at different times of the day (one with breakfast, one with dinner) because it helps break down the iron. Since iron has some other side effect like constipation, I also eat 4-5 dried plums / prunes each day with one of my iron pills, and it has really helped keep everything moving. These fruits also have the benefit of being high in nutrients. I will be 34 weeks with my triplets this week, and my blood work has come back with very steady (and high for triplets) iron levels, so it seems to be working. I have followed my doctor's suggestions and also the diet in Dr. Barbara Luke's pretty religiously."

"I am 30 1/2 weeks pregnant with triplets and had no problems until this week when my labs showed I had undetectable levels of vitamin B12 and I am severely anemic. My blood pressure is also high now, so I am hospitalized until birth. I had to have an IV of iron and take daily shots of B12. I have a week to get my red blood cells up to avoid a blood transfusion during delivery. I was taking a prescribed prenatal vitamin that included DHA, an important supplement for my babies' brain development. However, after we discovered my serious deficiencies, we checked the bottle and realized that my prenatal vitamin had no vitamin B12. Everything was great throughout my pregnancy until the babies doubled their weight last month and started tapping my reserve. That was when the problem arose. My advice is to take your vitamins to your doctors and ask them to make sure you are getting everything you need."

Anemia during a higher-order multiple pregnancy is very common and is present in almost 80% of all pregnant women. Because the volume of blood increases during pregnancy, a moderate decrease in the concentration of red blood cells and hemoglobin is normal. Iron deficiency is responsible for 95% of anemia of pregnancy. Causes of anemia include a diet without enough iron-rich foods, iron absorption problems or folic acid deficiency. Common symptoms of anemia include tiredness, weakness, fainting, paleness and breathlessness. On some occasions anemia can also cause headaches, nausea, an inflamed tongue, heart palpitations, forgetfulness and, in rare cases, jaundice or abdominal pain. Treatment includes eating a diet rich in iron, prenatal vitamins and/or folic acid supplements. Some expectant mothers also take ferrous sulfate medications (iron supplements), or in the case of iron absorption problems, iron injections. If your doctor recommends iron supplements, request that he recommend a time-release brand. You may also want to request a natural stool softener at this time in order to avoid constipation that is sometimes caused by an iron supplement. Because a multiple birth pregnancy is a risk factor for anemia, expectant mothers of multiples should be tested periodically for anemia and treated if indicated. Anemia can increase the likelihood of preterm labor, severe anemia immediately following delivery and susceptibility to infection after delivery.

Carpal Tunnel Syndrome

Carpal tunnel syndrome (CTS) occurs when a nerve (called the median nerve) is squeezed by excess fluid in the wrist. The nerve travels through the "tunnel" of the wrist bones and becomes compressed by tendons that also run through this area called the carpal tunnel. Around 20-30% of all expectant mothers develop CTS, and mothers expecting higher-order multiples may develop this condition more often due to the additional increase of fluid retention with multiple babies. Symptoms can include numbness, tingling, burning, and pain or a dull ache in the fingers, hand, wrist and even up the arm to the shoulder. In severe cases the hand may feel clumsy or weak. Symptoms usually affect both hands and can appear at any time but are more likely to begin or worsen during the second half of pregnancy when the mother retains more fluid. If you develop CTS, you should avoid any activity that requires forceful, repetitive hand movements that can make symptoms worse. Treatment often involves wearing wrist or hand braces and resting the hand in a neutral position. Acupuncture or local steroid injections may also help. If symptoms seem worse at night, you may want to try shifting your sleeping position, propping up your arm with a pillow or two, and avoiding sleeping on your hands. The symptoms usually go away gradually after giving birth as the swelling from pregnancy subsides.

Round Ligament Stretching

A sharp pain upon rolling over or standing up is common at around 10-12 weeks and then again about 22 weeks. This sharp pain goes from hip bone to pubic bone. This is normal and to be expected in any pregnancy but of course in a higher-order multiple pregnancy it may be a bit more noticeable. Talk with your doctor about possible treatments. The pain usually diminishes and disappears.

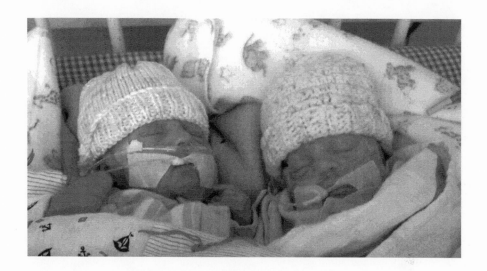

Twin-to-Twin Transfusion Syndrome

"Two of my babies developed Twin-to-Twin Transfusion Syndrome at about 23 weeks, but my doctors were able to get me to 30 weeks before delivering."

As mentioned earlier in this book, Twin-to-Twin Transfusion Syndrome (TTTS) is rare and only affects approximately 10% of all monochorionic pregnancies in the United States, which amounts to only about 2,000 pregnancies per year. [18] TTTS is even less common in higher-order multiple pregnancies than twin pregnancies since more twin pregnancies involve identical multiples than triplet or more pregnancies. TTTS occurs when the babies' placentas do not form correctly. This is a complex and serious complication. MOST recommends that families who have been diagnosed with TTTS contact reputable resources on this issue. [See resources at the end of this chapter.]

Definitions Related to TTTS

- **Amnion** – inner fetal membrane forming the sac that contains the fetus and fluid.

- **Chorion** – fetal membrane closest to the intrauterine wall and gives rise to the placenta.

- **Diamniotic-Dichorionic** – when the split happens within 3 days of conception, while the original zygote is still traveling down the fallopian tube, these identical twins will have two separate placentas, two chorions and two amnions.

- **Diamniotic-Monochorionic** – when division of the zygote occurs 4-7 days after conception, the twins will have separate amnions but will share one chorion and their placentas will be fused. Diamniotic/Monochorionic twins have the greatest risk of developing TTTS because they are sharing or have a fused placenta yet they have separate amniotic sacs.

- **Monoamniotic**/Monochorionic – when the split occurs after the 8th day following conception, the identical twins will share the same placenta, chorion and amnion.

- **Oligohydramnios** – decreased to no amniotic fluid.

- **Polyhydramnios** – excess amniotic fluid.

- **Zygosity** – one egg and one sperm unite to become a zygote. If the zygote divides there will be identical (monozygotic) twins; if one of them divides again, identical triplets, and if one divides again, identical quadruplets.

Symptoms of TTTS

Symptoms of TTTS include the mother exhibiting excessive weight gain, sudden growth of womb or severe swelling, but most frequently the mother experiences no symptoms, and TTTS is found via ultrasound. Ultrasound may reveal an increase in fluid around one identical twin and less or no fluid around the other as well as size differences in the identical babies. TTTS is usually found in the second trimester and can lead to PROM, preterm labor or possible fetal demise due to heart failure of one of the fetuses. In TTTS, a monochorionic placenta may cause greater flow of blood to one twin at the expense of the other due to a malformation of the placental blood vessels causing one twin to essentially "transfuse" the other. The decreased blood supply causes the internal organs of the donor twin to shut down (kidneys usually shut down first) causing a reduction in urine output and less amniotic fluid (oligohydramnios). This twin can become anemic, fail to grow properly and appears "stuck" to one spot in the uterus due to lack of amniotic fluid. The recipient twin produces excessive urine and therefore has a large volume of amniotic fluid (polyhydramnios). The recipient twin may be much larger and be surrounded by too much amniotic fluid, which can overwork his or her internal organs.

Treatment of TTTS

- **Delivery** – may not be an option until viability is obtained at 24-25 weeks. The physician must monitor the babies' situation very closely to determine optimal timing for delivery (e.g., when the risk of death outweighs the risk of premature birth.)

- **Septostomy** – a surgical procedure where numerous holes are made in the dividing membrane to equalize the pressure between the amniotic sacs making this a "pseudo mono-amniotic" twin pregnancy. This technique improves the amniotic fluid volume but does not solve the urinary output problem for either fetus. Once this surgery has been done other therapies are no longer an option.

- **Amnio-reduction** – or serial amniocentesis is a procedure where fluid is removed from the amniotic sac of the recipient twin to decrease pressure. Sometimes the mother is pre-medicated with a sedative to relax her and decrease fetal movement in the recipient twin. A needle is inserted into mother's abdomen carefully avoiding the placenta(s). The procedure is repeated numerous times during pregnancy, and again only treats the symptoms, not the blood vessel anomaly.

- **Laser therapy** – or fetoscopic laser occlusion of the connecting placental blood vessels (FLOC) is a surgical procedure where a thin fiber-optic scope is inserted through the mother's abdomen and the abnormal vessel connections are found and eliminated via laser beams to eliminate the blood exchange between the fetuses. This essentially gives each baby his or her own placenta. Although this procedure has been used since 1988 and has become more prevalent since 1995, currently only a few medical facilities and physicians perform this laser therapy.

- **Radiofrequency** - used to occlude one connect vessel

Gestational Diabetes

"I just got my results back, and thank goodness I do not have gestational diabetes! I was close, but I passed. I am so relieved. At my appointment today the doctors and nurses commented on how pleased they were with my progress and the fact that I am not in the hospital. I am on cloud 9, so I guess that is proof "this too shall pass" works! Thanks MOST for getting me through the rough spot. I know I will have many ups and downs in the weeks to come but will try to remember the good that is around the corner."

Gestational diabetes is characterized by high blood sugar (glucose) levels during pregnancy in a non-diabetic person. The exact cause is unknown, but weight gain could be a contributor and the hormones from the placenta (or placentas) may block the action of the mother's insulin (a hormone made by the pancreas) causing her to need up to 3 times more insulin than usual.

Without insulin, glucose cannot be removed from the bloodstream by the cells to be used as fuel for the body; therefore, the blood contains a high level of blood sugar or glucose (hyperglycemia) which can cause damage to vital organs like the eyes and kidneys. Usually you will have a fasting glucose tolerance test sometime between 22-26 weeks gestation. It may be earlier if your physician has concerns.

Symptoms of Gestational Diabetes

- Excessive thirst or hunger
- Unusual frequency of urination

- Glucose noted on urine sample at physician's office
- You may feel no symptoms which is why doctors test for this

Gestational diabetes affects only about 4% of all pregnant women and is 2 to 3 times more prevalent during a multiple gestation. Gestational diabetes differs from other diabetes because it does not affect the mother until later in the pregnancy when the babies are already formed; therefore, the effect on the babies is not as severe as might be in a woman with Type I or II diabetes.

Treatment for gestational diabetes may involve diet restrictions, exercise if allowed, daily monitoring of glucose levels, urine checks for ketones (a chemical made when blood sugar levels increase causing the body to burn fat instead of sugar for energy), oral medications like Metformin and in some cases, insulin injections. A link between having gestational diabetes in subsequent pregnancies may exist if diagnosed in a previous pregnancy. In addition, the chance of developing Type II diabetes later in life may be greater in women who have gestational diabetes. Gestational diabetes generally goes away after delivery.

Skin Changes During Pregnancy

You have most likely read about the typical skin problems and concerns during pregnancy such as acne, dark blotches on the face ("mask of pregnancy"), linea nigra, stretch marks and unusual rashes. Pregnancy can cause other effects on your skin such as dry skin, sensitivity to sunlight, skin bumps, skin tags, tender belly button, and itchy palms and soles of your feet. Let your doctor know if you have very itchy palms and soles as this may indicate cholestasis of pregnancy, a common liver condition during pregnancy.

Split skin may actually occur on your abdomen due to the excessive stretching of your skin. You might need to try a few things to see what brings you relief. Some women find rubbing oil (olive oil or no additive skin oil) or lotion on the skin and placing plastic wrap across the area helped ease the tenderness. Other women find a cold compress to help. In extreme circumstances, bandages or cloths may be needed to absorb oozing fluids. Keeping the skin clean and moisturized may help prevent split skin and you may need medications to help heal.

These skin conditions usually resolve soon after delivery.

Hypertension, Preeclampsia, Toxemia, Pregnancy-Induced Hypertension (PIH)

All these terms have almost the same meaning, so you may hear any or all of them. Mothers pregnant with multiples are more likely to develop problems with blood pressure. The MOST Medical Birth survey showed that over 32% of respondents developed PIH. To minimize problems your blood pressure and the presence of protein in your urine (by urine sample) will be checked frequently through your pregnancy. If your blood pressure is elevated to 140/90 or above you may be told you have Pregnancy-Induced Hypertension (PIH). However, if you have elevated blood pressure and protein in your urine (proteinurea) then you most likely have preeclampsia. Preeclampsia used to be called toxemia. Your doctor will be following you closely if you develop high blood pressure; however, call your doctor or nurse right away if any of these symptoms suddenly occur.

- Fluid retention
- Swelling or puffiness of the hands, feet and face - usually noted in the morning
- Rapid weight gain
- Dizziness
- Headaches that are not relieved by taking allowed medications like Tylenol
- Blurry vision or seeing "spots" or flashing lights before eyes
- Infrequent urination or inability to urinate
- Pain in the upper right abdomen (Abdominal cramping or severe pain, with or without bleeding, can possibly indicate the placenta has separated from the wall of the uterus which is an **emergency**.)

The causes of PIH are not known but thought to be an immunologic reaction to the pregnancy where the mother's body interprets the baby as a foreign tissue. This complication usually occurs during the second half of the pregnancy and is more common in pregnancies with multiples and mothers over the age of 40. Women with diabetes, teenagers, women over 40-years-old and women who have had high blood pressure or kidney disease are also at a higher risk of developing PIH.

Twenty-four hour urine protein tests, blood tests for liver and kidney problems and coagulation studies are used to diagnose PIH. Treatment options include bedrest, diet restrictions (low/ no salt diet), peace and quiet and medication to lower blood pressure; however, childbirth is the only cure.

HELLP Syndrome

HELLP syndrome is a severe form of gestational hypertension and stands for Hemolysis (breaking down of the red blood cells), Elevated Liver Enzymes, Low Platelet count (platelets help blood coagulate). Symptoms of HELLP syndrome include headache, nausea, vomiting or right upper abdominal pain or tenderness (from liver distention). The mother may or may not experience a severe headache, bleeding, visual disturbances, swelling, high blood pressure or protein in her urine. This is not a common complication but can occur.

HELLP can cause anemia and blood clotting problems such as disseminated intravascular coagulation (DIC) which leads to severe bleeding or hemorrhage, placental abruption (an early detachment of the placenta), or pulmonary edema (a buildup of fluid in the lungs). Treatment is similar to PIH.

Poor Fetal Growth (Fetal Growth Restriction)

"I had one triplet measuring 5 days behind the others the whole pregnancy. She was only 3 ounces smaller at birth. Hang in there – eat – enjoy!"

Poor fetal growth is called fetal growth restriction or retardation (FGR), previously called intrauterine growth restriction or retardation (IUGR). This means that a baby weighs at least 10% less than normal for that gestational age. At birth these babies may be called small for gestational age (SGA). The diagnosis of FGR is unusual but not unheard of. The diagnosis is made by ultrasound measurements of the baby. Not all of your babies may be diagnosed with FGR; most likely only one will be. Common causes of FGR include placental problems like TTTS, birth defects, genetic disorders, poor nutrition, maternal infections, high blood pressure, smoking, alcohol consumption or drugs (even prescription medications). There may not be any preventable reason for FGR occurring. Treatment will depend on the cause, if known, for the poor fetal growth. Once diagnosed with FGR your babies will be monitored even more closely. Some doctors will increase your bedrest, increase your calorie intake, provide supplemental oxygen and/or prescribe hydrotherapy (immersion in a therapy pool in the hospital or in a swimming pool while home). Sometimes the babies need to be delivered and your doctor should discuss the various possibilities with you.

Babies with FGR may be weak, have tissue and organs that fail to grow as large as expected and may possibly experience long-term effects such as learning disabilities. However, other babies may be small since conception and continue to grow at their own steady rate throughout the pregnancy and may always be small but reach developmental milestones on time and not have any long lasting problems. This is especially true if both parents are small in stature.

PUPPP

"I soaked my feet in a bucket of ice until they were numb then lightly patted them dry. Finally, I lightly coated them with petroleum jelly and wrapped them in plastic wrap (like Saran wrap). It worked to stop the itching and get me through the night."

Pruitic Urticarial Papules and Plaques of Pregnancy (PUPP or PUPPP) is an itchy hive-like rash, which starts on the abdomen near stretch marks, and then can spread to the thighs, buttocks and sometimes arms. PUPPP is harmless to the mother and babies and is thought to be caused by the stretching of the skin, which creates an inflammatory reaction causing it to spread.

PUPPP generally occurs during the second half of pregnancy in only a small number of pregnant women and goes away a few days after delivery. It seldom occurs in subsequent pregnancies and is less severe if it does. The mother needs to get a definite diagnosis of PUPPP before treatment, as there are other rashes associated with pregnancy that may require a different treatment. The doctor may prescribe a topical ointment, and in severe cases medication, usually a steroid. Heat increases the itching, so cold baths and showers, a non-scented moisturizer or applying a cloth soaked in cold water helps.

Vaginal Bleeding

"I had dark red bleeding and brown spotting from week 4 through 14 weeks. At 17 weeks I had a significant bleeding episode. My perinatologist could not find the source of the bleeding with ultrasound but speculated that it was a placenta moving or tearing a bit from the uterus. The bleeding stopped with bedrest and my perinatologists were comfortable with this. I was still worried all the time, especially when I would go to the bathroom, so I understand the anxiety of this happening. I think that bleeding/spotting during pregnancy is very common with multiples since there is a lot going on in your uterus."

Twenty-five percent of all women have vaginal bleeding during the first 16 weeks of pregnancy. Sometimes there is a small amount of bleeding when a fertilized egg implants (between 4-6 weeks), which may be heavier due to multiple eggs implanting. Other expectant mothers, especially those who have used ART, may experience this when the placentas begin to attach to the lining of the uterus between 8-11 weeks. Bleeding may also be due to an incompetent cervix early in the pregnancy.

Another cause can be a subchorionic hematoma/hemorrhage that is also not uncommon after ART. A subchorionic hematoma is a blood clot that collects between the uterine wall and the chorionic sac that can be seen on ultrasound. This condition usually disappears without incident but might present a danger to the fetuses due to decreased blood flow. The more the placenta separates from the uterine wall, the more serious the problem. In addition, a larger size hematoma may also result in less blood flow to one or more babies. Treatment may include bedrest, prohibiting heavy lifting (nothing heavier than a gallon of milk), pelvic rest (no sex or vaginal ultrasound) and avoiding constipation.

The source of bleeding after the 20th week of pregnancy is usually the placenta, and is more common in a multiple pregnancy due to the increased number of placentas. The bleeding is generally caused by one these three factors.

- **Abruptio Placenta (Placental Abruption)** - is very rare and occurs when the placenta partially detaches from the uterus before delivery. Symptoms include moderate to heavy bleeding or moderate to severe abdominal pain.

- **Placenta Previa** - occurs when a placenta implants low in the uterus and either partially or completely covers the cervix. This condition is common in a multiple pregnancy due to the increased number of placentas. Generally, by 22 weeks this resolves as the placenta moves further and further away from the cervix (although it is not actually "moving" at all). Think of your cervix and uterus as a balloon, with the cervix being the neck of the balloon. As you fill up the balloon the neck gets shorter and shorter and what was once right at the opening is being pushed further and further from the neck as the neck gets shorter. Just as with the balloon, what was once right at the opening of the cervix is stretched further and further away as your uterus expands.

- **Cervical Dilation** - vaginal bleeding may occur as the cervix begins to open toward the end of the pregnancy.

As noted earlier, if you ever go to the hospital because of a vaginal discharge take your soiled underwear with you in a sealable plastic bag. This may provide important information to your health care provider.

Preterm Premature Rupture of Membranes (PPROM)

The term "rupture of the membranes" refers to a tear or rip in the amniotic sac. If it occurs before 37 weeks gestation it is called preterm premature rupture of membranes (PPROM). If it occurs after 37 weeks gestation but prior to labor then it is referred to premature rupture of the membranes (PROM). For the vast majority of higher-order multiple births a tear in the amniotic sac will be considered PPROM. The primary symptom of PPROM will be fluid leaking from the vagina, which can take the form of a sudden gush or slow trickle. This can be hard for an expectant mother to figure out since it may seem as her pregnancy progresses that all she has to do is laugh, cough or sneeze and there is a little trickle of some liquid between her legs. After about 16 weeks gestation you may want to wear a mini-pad all the time for just this reason. Most likely it is urine, but if you ever have ANY questions do not hesitate to call your doctor. If it is actually PPROM, labor generally begins within 24 hours of the membranes rupturing. Expectant mothers who have any of the following risk factors may be more likely to experience PPROM:

- Smoking
- Multiple pregnancy
- Infection
- Polyhydramnios (excess amniotic fluid)
- Placental abruption
- Procedures such as an amniocentesis

The diagnostic tests used to determine if the membranes have ruptured include a cervical exam to check for leaking or pooling of fluid (doctors claim it has a "musty smell") and using nitrazine paper that will turn from yellowish green to dark blue if amniotic fluid is present. A microscopic slide with the dried liquid appears "feathery" like a fern when the membranes have ruptured. Ultrasound can be used as well to diagnose PPROM where decreased or no amniotic fluid is observed.

Treatment depends on time of occurrence and may include tocolytics (medications to stop or control contractions to delay preterm labor) and/or steroids to mature babies' lungs. Antibiotics may be used if the doctors are worried about the mother developing an infection or if infection is suspected such as when the mother has a fever, pain, an elevated white blood cell count, vaginal discharge, or if the babies have an increased heart rate. Hospitalization for close observation of mother and babies may be required; however, sometimes a small leak will seal itself.

Losses during Pregnancy

"When I learned that we were not carrying quadruplets but rather quintuplets all I could think was, what are we going to do with another baby? How on earth are we going to be able to manage? When we lost our dearest Zachary later in the pregnancy all I could think was, what are we going to do without this baby? How on earth are we going to be able to manage?"

Unfortunately, sometimes a pregnancy does not result in a live birth. With more than one baby, there is a chance that a baby may die while still in the womb prior to birth. If a loss occurs before 20 weeks gestation, it is referred to as a miscarriage. Miscarriage is fairly common during any pregnancy and the loss can occur even before the woman is aware she is pregnant. The risk is slightly higher in a multiple pregnancy. Many miscarriages have no determined cause. Sometimes all the babies are miscarried; in other situations only one (or more) of the babies will be lost and the other babies will continue to grow and thrive. Almost all miscarriages occur before the 12th week of pregnancy, and most of the remaining losses occur before the 16th week of pregnancy.

While the definition of stillbirth varies around the world, including the US, it is generally understood to be the death of a baby in utero, prior to or during birth that occurs after 20 weeks gestation. The baby is born 'still', showing no signs of life.

Stillbirth occurs in approximately 6 of every 1000 pregnancies with a small percentage of stillbirths occurring during labor and delivery and the majority occurring just before labor begins. [16] Multiple gestation pregnancies have an increased incidence of stillbirth, especially higher-order multiple pregnancies that progress beyond 38 weeks gestation. [17] In 1/3 of pregnancies involving a stillbirth, no cause is determined. MOST strongly recommends you discuss with your doctor how long he/she will allow your pregnancy to go. Most triplet pregnancies will be delivered by 36 completed weeks and quadruplets by 34 completed weeks in order to decrease the risk of stillbirth among other reasons.

When a baby dies in-utero during a multiple birth pregnancy, parents may go through weeks or months of pregnancy hoping to have at least one survivor delivered as close to term as possible. We suggest that parents request as many sonogram printouts of all of the babies seen together on the same screen as possible. For some parents these may be their only photo of all of their children together. To maintain the uniqueness of multiples parents may want to request a picture of all the babies together after delivery if possible, even after one or more babies has died. Although parents may not wish to see the photo soon after delivery, they sometimes want to see it in the future. Many have said that they treasure this small gift. Photos are also suggested following a stillbirth when parents are usually trying to deal with the loss of one or more babies while also coping with one or more babies struggling to live in the

NICU. A professional non-profit photographer group called *Now I Lay Me Down to Sleep* (see resources at the end of this chapter) provides free professional photographs of stillborn or newborn babies who die. Parents may also wish to request the baby's hospital items to keep in memory boxes for themselves and each of the baby's siblings, so that they may treasure these items that were part of their life.

Many health care providers recommend parents see and hold their baby after a loss, but each family will have to make their own decision about this. Some families name the baby and feel comforted by referring to him/her by name as well as asking the medical team to consider doing the same. Many parents include the child's name in their birth announcements as a way to share their joy and their loss. You may even want to consider having a memorial service at the same time you are having a naming or baptism for your other babies so that he/she will be remembered and a part of this special moment as well.

Parents often feel "special" to be expecting twins, triplets or more, so when one or more babies suddenly dies, some parents may feel "un-chosen". People may say, "You can always have another baby" but they almost never say "You could always try to have triplets again." In addition, parents will forever be faced with the questions "Are they twins?" or "Are they triplets?"

For most parents the loss of a multiple during or after pregnancy involves a complex grieving process. The loss of one or more babies while continuing a pregnancy can be a very emotional experience. There is no right or wrong way to incorporate this into your lives. The resources listed by MOST at the end of this chapter, especially the Center for Loss in Multiple Birth (CLIMB), have more information on this topic. The question of how to address the surviving multiple(s) is a personal choice that may evolve over a long period. Some parents choose to call their LIVING children "surviving triplets," "surviving quadruplets," etc. For example, when one triplet does not survive pregnancy or birth, the other two may be referred to as "surviving triplets." Unfortunately, the public usually does not understand an answer like "surviving triplets" or "surviving quintuplets" so this answer may lead to additional painful and distressing questions. Other families, for various reasons, prefer to call two surviving multiples "twins," three surviving multiples "triplets," etc. While this approach may seem like an easier option, many parents feel that this answer is slighting the baby(ies) who did not survive. Every family needs to choose what is right for them at the time because the choice of wording may change over time. From a medical perspective, doctors must document the birth based on reporting requirements, but physicians can be asked to refer to a set of survivors based the parent's preferences and will usually support whatever option a parent chooses. If you experience a loss, let your pediatrician and the office staff know how you would like the survivors to be addressed.

Effects of Early Partial Loss

A loss of one or more, but not all, babies prior to 16 weeks is called an early partial loss. Sometimes the loss occurs shortly after finding out you are expecting multiples, and you may only be aware of the partial loss due to an ultrasound performed early in pregnancy. Even though a heartbeat may be seen, the baby stops developing. When one or more babies stop growing and vanish, this is called a spontaneous reabsorption, but you may also hear the phrase "vanishing twin." The baby does not vanish; it is absorbed by the mother's placenta and can no longer be seen. Early losses are considered fairly common occurrences with all pregnancies and are not due to anything you did or did not do. Whether a loss occurs early or late in the pregnancy, you can choose to refer to the remaining babies as "surviving multiples" or by how many are continuing to develop. Since there is no right or wrong answer, you should use the term that is most comfortable for you.

Effects of Complete Loss

You will likely experience some physical and emotional effects if all of your babies die early in the pregnancy. Your doctor will guide you on how much time your body will need to recover and what you can do to help yourself recover physically. The recovery will depend on the gestational age of your babies when they died. Your doctor will guide you toward the next step. For example, you may need a dilation and curettage (D&C) to remove all the tissue from the pregnancy. If your babies die later in your pregnancy, your doctor might suggest dilation and evacuation (D&E) or an induction of labor to delivery your babies vaginally. If you deliver vaginally, many parents find comfort in holding their babies in a warm blanket. You may want to take pictures of your babies separately and together and ask your nurse to make footprints for a memory box.

Your breasts may continue to be tender and full for a while, and some women produce breast milk. The abdomen will lose its fullness gradually as the uterus contracts. The return of normal menstruation may vary, and the abrupt hormonal changes may cause mood swings and exhaustion. Overall it may take several weeks for your body to adjust to not being pregnant.

Your physical body may heal before your emotional state recovers. Seeking help to deal with your feelings and grief is useful for many. Talking about your loss is usually important. Your partner may have different feelings about the loss, but this is not uncommon since people, even couples in a very loving relationship, deal with loss and grief in various ways. Please contact the MOST office for support and referral.

Effects of Late Partial Loss

As mentioned earlier in this book, stillbirth refers to the death of a fetus at any time after the 20th week of pregnancy. Stillbirth is also referred to as intrauterine fetal death (IUFD). A late partial loss occurs when one or more babies dies in-utero before delivery or are born too early to survive (less than 24 weeks gestation) while one or more baby(ies) continue to grow in the uterus. Partial losses can increase risk to a pregnancy including an earlier delivery of the surviving baby(ies), infection, blood clot or loss of entire pregnancy.

After a late partial loss is discovered the mother and remaining babies are watched closely for about 3 days for possible signs of labor. If this does not occur, her body is accepting the changes and the pregnancy continues as previously expected. If the mother experiences cervical changes or funneling, she may go into labor or have increased uterine activity. If the mother's amniotic sac ruptures, she will have to be monitored very closely since she would then be considered at risk for developing an infection that may spread to one or more babies making delivery imminent. If the baby who dies is positioned lowest in the uterus, the doctor may consider a Delayed Interval Delivery (DID) if the mother shows no signs of infection. [See chapter 8 for more information about DID.]

The loss of one baby in monochorionic (identical twins with a shared placenta) pregnancies can also result in the death of the co-twin about 35% of the time. [13] When a monochorionic twin dies in-utero, the other baby or babies must be watched closely for signs of possible organ damage.

Emotionally some mothers struggle to continue with a pregnancy when one or more babies die. However, if your body can continue the pregnancy and your doctors agree, the remaining babies have the best chance of being healthy if the pregnancy continues to a later gestation. MOST wants all families to know that if you started your pregnancy as a multiple birth, you will forever be a part of the MOST family. We were there for you at the beginning of your journey, and we are here for you now and every step of the way.

References

(16) MacDorman MF, Kirmeyer S. Fetal and perinatal mortality, United States, 2005. National vital statistics reports; vol 57 no 8. Hyattsville, MD: National Center for Health Statistics. 2009. http://www.cdc.gov/nchs/data/nvsr/nvsr57/nvsr57_08.pdf (accessed June 22, 2012).

(17) Sairam, S, K Costeloe, and B Thilaganathan. "Prospective Risk of Stillbirth in Multiple Gestation Pregnancies: A Population-based Analysis." *Obstetrics & Gynecology* 100 (2002): 638-641

(18) Quintero, R A, C Comas, P W Bornick, and et al. "Selective versus Non-selective Laser Photocoagulation of Placental Vessels in Twin-to-Twin Transfusion Syndrome." *Ultrasound in Obstetrics & Gynecology* 16 (2000): 230-236.

Resources

Hyperemesis

- Hyperemesis Education Resource or the HER Foundation is the leading site for Hyperemesis Gravidarum information on the Internet: http://www.helpher.org/

- *No More Morning Sickness: A Survival Guide for Pregnant Women* by Miriam Erick

- WebMD Pregnancy Forum: Severe Morning Sickness Topic http://forums.webmd.com/3/pregnancy-exchange/forum/4812

Anemia

- WebMD Guide to Iron Deficiency Anemia: www.webmd.com/a-to-z-guides/iron-deficiency-anemia-topic-overview

- American Society of Hematology: http://www.hematology.org/patients/blood-disorders/anemia/5227.aspx

Carpal Tunnel Syndrome

- National Institutes of Neurological Disorders and Stroke fact sheet: www.ninds.nih.gov/disorders/carpal_tunnel/carpal_tunnel.htm
- American Society for Surgery of the Hand Carpal Tunnel Syndrome FAQs: www.assh.org/Public/HandConditions/Pages/CubitalTunnelSyndrome.aspx

Twin-to-Twin Transfusion Syndrome

- Twin-to-Twin Transfusion Syndrome Foundation: www.tttsfoundation.org or 1-800-815-9211

Preeclampsia

- National American Society for the Study of Hypertension in Pregnancy (NASSHP): www.nasshp.org
- Preeclampsia Foundation: info@preeclampsia.org, www.preeclampsia.org, or 1-800-665-9341

Loss during Pregnancy

- MOST offers personal support to multiple birth families that experience a loss during or after pregnancy as well as our Multiple Loss Bereavement Booklet (free to any family who experiences the loss of one of more of their multiples). Visit the MOST Memorial page for more information: www.MOSTonline.org/memorialview.html
- Center for Loss in Multiple Births (CLIMB): www.climb-support.org
- Now I Lay Me Down to Sleep is a non-profit organization that connects families with professional photographers who volunteer their time to capture final moments in what is known as remembrance photography: www.nowilaymedowntosleep.org
- Share Pregnancy and Infant Loss Support, Inc. (chapters in many states): www.nationalshare.org/

- Stillbirth and Neonatal Death Support (SANDS) (chapters in UK, Australia and USA): www.uk-sands.org

Chapter 5: Tests and Treatments

Photo by Main Street Studio & Gallery Inc.

S ome of these tests and treatments will definitely be performed during your pregnancy while other tests may not be needed. Your doctor can explain why he performs or recommends some tests and treatment as well as why he does not recommend others.

Ultrasounds and Biophysical Profiles (BPP)

Ultrasounds

Ultrasound (US) waves are used to show "pictures" of the babies, the amniotic fluid surrounding them, the membranes separating them, the placenta or placentas and the length of the cervix. Fully evaluating each individual fetus can be difficult in a multiple pregnancy, so ultrasound examinations should be performed by a skilled technician who has experience with multiples. Many MFM specialists perform their own ultrasounds. You will most likely have more ultrasounds during your multiple pregnancy than during a singleton pregnancy. Be sure to bring your pregnancy notebook with you and write down any questions you may have. Inquire as to whether asking questions during this exam is appropriate or if you should wait until after it is completed. If your doctor is not performing the exam, inquire about whether you should wait to discuss questions with your doctor directly.

Frequency of Ultrasound Tests

The frequency of ultrasound tests varies among physicians. Ultrasounds may be done more often and earlier if infertility procedures were used to achieve a pregnancy. A typical schedule for ultrasounds in an uncomplicated higher-order multiple pregnancy might be as follows:

- At 5-6 weeks a scan is done by the infertility specialist or OB-GYN.

- At 8-10 weeks a quick scan is done to check the heartbeats and placentas.

- At 12 weeks a more in-depth ultrasound may be done during your consult with a perinatologist or high-risk specialist.

- Around 18-20 weeks a Level II (comprehensive) ultrasound is done by the Maternal-Fetal Medicine specialist, which may take from ½-1 hour depending on how many babies you are expecting.

- Around 22 weeks a second Level II ultrasound may be done, which may take from 45 minutes - 1½ hours. Bring a snack, water bottle and a pillow for comfort. Ask if you can take a break or sit up if you feel you need to.

- Around 26-28 weeks a modified or baseline Biophysical Profile (BPP) is done, which may take 1-2 hours.

- After 24 or 26 weeks ultrasounds are done about every 3-4 weeks although some doctors may do a "quick scan" at every visit.

Additional ultrasounds may be performed should complications arise, and more frequent scans may be done from 28 weeks on if the physician suspects fetal growth restriction. It takes 3-4 weeks for a physician to see a statistical difference in the growth, so even though you may want these ultrasounds each week, the physician may not perform them that often.

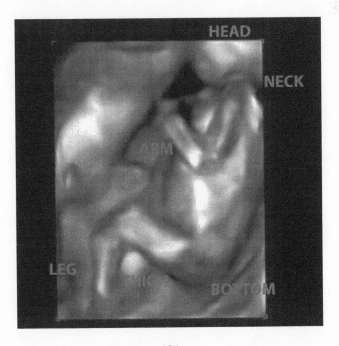

Ultrasound Types

Depending on what your doctor is looking for, different ultrasounds may be done. An abdominal ultrasound uses a wand and gel on the outside of the abdomen. A transvaginal ultrasound involves inserting a lubricated wand into the vagina. Some questions you may wish to ask during ultrasounds done from 12 weeks on include:

- Are the babies the same size as each other?

- Is each the same size as that of a singleton at the same gestation?

- How many placentas do I have?

- Is each placenta separate and distinct? After 16 weeks or so it is not uncommon for the placentas to fuse.

- Are any placentas low lying?

- Do any of the babies have too much or too little amniotic fluid?

About 18-20 weeks into your pregnancy a Level II ultrasound is done. Sometimes this is referred to as a detailed complete ultrasound or comprehensive ultrasound. This is a detailed fetal survey to check each baby's organs, bone growth and placentas. This test should be performed using the most advanced equipment by a skilled technician. Your doctor goes into the exam looking for specific information, so if you have ANY congenital concerns, ask your doctor if he would be able to rule this out at this, or at a later, exam. This can be a time when you cross off one or two concerns from your list of worries that you may have. Your doctor will usually just say that everyone looks fine, but what he is really telling you is that as far as he can tell at this point, the babies have no obvious congenital abnormalities and that everyone looks PERFECT. He has looked at everyone's spine, kidneys, long bones, brain, heart and much more! Before you deliver, you could possibly know almost everything, other than eye color, about each of your babies. What a HUGE gift! Women in a singleton, non-high-risk pregnancy may never know all of this until after they deliver.

A Biophysical Profile (BPP combines an ultrasound with a non-stress test and is highly recommended in a multiple gestation. It is a simple, painless test used to assess whether the babies are getting enough oxygen. The test is typically performed at 26, 28 and/or 32 weeks during a higher-order multiple pregnancy and may be repeated twice a week. The BPP may be done if the doctor has a concern about the development of one or more babies. The test presents no known risks to either the mother or babies. Usually you need to have a full bladder for this test, but sometimes that is not necessary later in the pregnancy. You will need to lie on a table that may be uncomfortable. Let your health care provider know if you are uncomfortable and/or become faint from lying down. The BPP is much like other external abdominal ultrasounds you have already had to this point.

The BPP consists of a detailed ultrasound to observe five areas:

1. The babies' body movements

2. Muscle tone

3. Movements of the chest muscles and diaphragm

4. Amniotic fluid level

5. A non-stress test to assess the babies' heart rate changes while moving

Each of the five areas is assigned a score of either 0 (abnormal) or 2 (normal). These scores are added for a total score ranging from 0 to 10. In general a total score of 8 to 10 is normal, 6 is considered borderline and below 6 is worrisome. Depending on each baby's BPP score, your practitioner may recommend further testing such as a Doppler ultrasound study. The Doppler flow, or Doppler velocimetry, is a type of ultrasound that measures the flow of blood through a blood vessel. A specially trained physician performs an abdominal ultrasound using a specialized machine. The test takes several minutes to assess the blood flow and is not harmful to mother or baby.

A Doppler flow ultrasound is used to assess blood flow in the umbilical arteries, babies' brains and hearts and is often used when one or more babies show signs of Intrauterine Growth Restriction (IUGR). Waveforms may show that the blood flow in the umbilical vessels of a baby with IUGR is decreased. This indicates that the baby is not receiving enough blood, nutrients and oxygen from the placenta.

Reasons for Conducting an Ultrasound

1. Check for number of fetuses
2. Determine due date
3. Measure each baby's growth
4. Check the volume of amniotic fluid
5. Identify and monitor any problems in each baby's organs and growth
6. Check the placental length and functioning (quality of the blood flow)
7. Check the length of the cervix later in pregnancy (shortening is a sign that there is a risk of preterm labor)
8. Use as a guide for certain procedures (e.g. amniocentesis)

Amniocentesis and Chorionic Villus Sampling

"We had a scare at 11 weeks from an ultrasound that showed an abnormal neck on Baby A. They called it Nuchal Translucency. I did not know what this was but it sounded horrifying. They told us that Baby A had a 1 in 2 chance of Down syndrome. We did a CVS on Baby A alone (I was scared about the risk of miscarriage so we did not test the other two). Everything turned out fine; our baby had no sign of chromosomal problems."

Amniocentesis

This test is generally not recommended for all pregnancies due to a chance of miscarriage. Amniocentesis is done typically between the 16th and 18th weeks to check for genetic disorders and possibly later, toward the end of the pregnancy, to ascertain lung maturity just before delivery. The procedure involves a thin needle inserted through the abdomen into the amniotic sac. The needle is guided via ultrasound and a small amount of amniotic fluid is withdrawn to check for genetic disorders or to determine lung maturity. This is done for each baby. The risks associated with amniocentesis include cramping, spotting, and a risk of miscarriage. This test should only be done by a skilled technician or physician in a triplet or more pregnancy! The results for genetic disorders are usually available in about 2 weeks.

Since there are risks associated with this test, you need to think about what you will do if the amniocentesis results are not favorable BEFORE undergoing the procedure and how you might feel about the options that could be presented. This is not a routine test in higher-order multiple pregnancies. Most women will find out that their baby or babies do not have the disorders that are screened by this test, but if your baby's (or babies') tests indicate a genetic disorder, your health care provider will guide you through your options.

Chorionic Villus Sampling

Chorionic Villus Sampling (CVS) involves removing a small sample of tissue from the placenta usually through the vagina. Sometimes this test is done through the abdomen much like an amniocentesis. This test detects genetic disorders such as Down syndrome, Tay-Sachs and sickle cell anemia, and is typically done only once between the 10th and 12th weeks of gestation. The risks associated with this test include cramping or spotting and a slight risk of miscarriage. Results are usually available within a week.

Since there is a risk of miscarriage, you need to think about what you will do if the results are not favorable BEFORE undergoing the procedure and how you might feel about the options that could be presented.

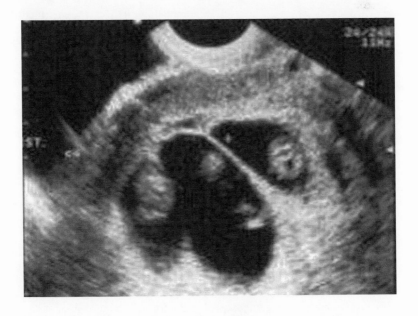

Corticosteroids

Corticosteroids are used to help the fetal lungs develop more quickly if the babies are going to be born before 34 weeks gestation. These drugs cause the baby to make surfactant which is needed for the lungs to work properly. Sometimes these medications are referred to as steroids and are generally not given until delivery appears imminent. To maximize the effect on the babies' lungs, the steroids need to be given two days prior to delivery and less than two weeks prior to delivery. A typical course includes two injections given to the mother 24 hours apart. The generic medications commonly used are dexamethasone and betamethasone (Celestone is the brand name). While research on use of these drugs continues, at this point in time, the benefits of these drugs outweigh the possible side effects which include:

- Sleeplessness
- Increased maternal blood sugar
- Increased movement in babies
- An increased risk of pulmonary edema when combined with tocolytics
- Increased anxiety
- Contractions for 24 hours after administration. Medications (tocolytics) may be needed to reduce the contractions.

Cerclage

"I had a cerclage at 13 weeks with my quadruplets. All of my doctors (one regular OB-GYN and 3 perinatologists) were a little skeptical about it being effective, but my Reproductive Endocrinologist scheduled and did it before these doctors were in the picture. My pregnancy lasted 33 weeks 2 days, and one of my perinatologists said he had become a believer. He now thought that the cerclage played an important part in my getting that far. Of course bedrest, diet and my amazing compliance as a patient were also factors!"

A cervical cerclage is a surgical procedure used to treat an incompetent cervix, which occurs in about 10% of higher-order multiple pregnancies. The cervix is at the lower end of the uterus and is the opening to the vagina. The cervix is called incompetent if it opens (dilates) before labor should begin. Women with an abnormality in the shape or structure of the cervix, who have had cervical procedures done such as LEEP or have a history of early preterm birth or pregnancy loss, are usually candidates for a cerclage. While some physicians do this procedure routinely around 14 weeks gestation for all higher-order multiple pregnancies, others perform a cerclage only on a case-by-case basis. To date, no conclusive studies support performing a routine elective cerclage for any multiples: twins, triplets, or more.

The procedure starts with testing for a urinary tract infection and bacterial vaginitis. Antibiotics will be given if necessary. The procedure is usually an outpatient procedure. Anesthesia is used while the physician sews the cervical opening closed like a purse string. The procedure works best when done early in pregnancy but may be performed at up to 22 to 23 weeks gestation in emergency circumstances. You may stay overnight to be monitored for contractions. Usually after a few days of limited activity, you can resume your regular activities. Check with your doctor to know your activity level guidelines. For a few days you may have light bleeding and mild cramping. Some women have an increased thick vaginal discharge, which may continue for the remainder of the pregnancy.

The risks associated with a cervical cerclage include contractions that may require tocolytics, infection of the cervix that may require antibiotics (symptoms of infection are fever, chills, foul smelling vaginal discharge), and in rare cases ruptured membranes or more bleeding than expected by your physician. In rare cases, the whole pregnancy is lost. The cerclage is not removed until delivery or at 37 gestation.

Pessary

Although not commonly used, sometimes a pessary can be part of the treatment plan to help prevent preterm delivery. A pessary is a rubber or plastic device (usually doughnut shaped) that is inserted by your doctor near the cervix. It fits around or under the cervix to help prop up the uterus and hold it in place. It is used as a mechanical means of supporting the cervix if you experience early dilation of the cervix. The pessary also works as a mechanical means of treating preterm labor by altering the pressure on the cervix, and is generally used with tocolytic medications.

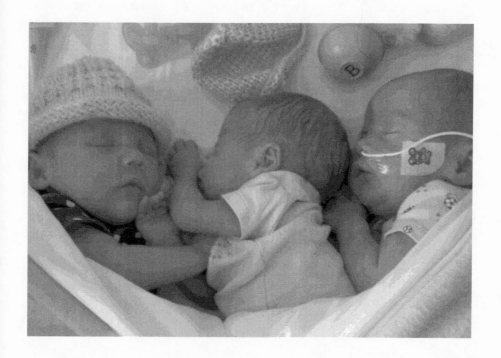

Chapter 6: Preterm Labor and Bedrest

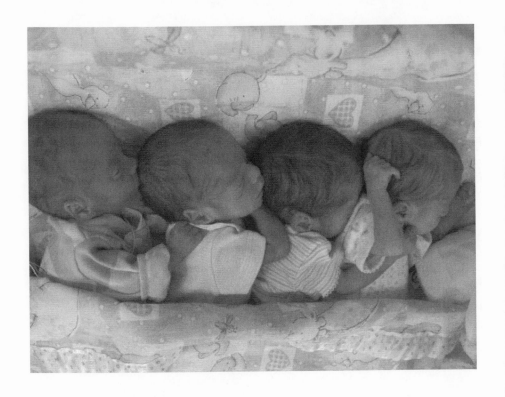

"I went into preterm labor at 23 weeks and was given medication that slowed down the contractions. The medication worked for several weeks. At 26 weeks I was in preterm labor once again and was now 2 cm. dilated. I was hospitalized, given medication to control the contractions and my pregnancy continued 6 more weeks. I had preterm labor that could not be controlled at 32 weeks and delivered 3 very wonderful, healthy preemies. I thought that since I started to dilate there was nothing that could be done and that I would deliver back at 26 weeks. I am so very grateful that my body responded to the medications, and we were able to get 6 more weeks."

Preterm Labor: What It Is

Preterm labor happens when the uterus contracts enough to cause the cervix to efface and dilate when the mother is less than 38 weeks into the pregnancy. If the uterus contracts but does not cause cervical change that is not called preterm labor. Effacing means the cervix is gradually softening, shortening and becoming thinner. Effacement is sometimes called "cervical thinning" or you might hear the phrase "the cervix is ripening." You might also hear effacement described in a percentage such as, "You are 25% effaced." When the cervix dilates, it opens which is described in centimeters such as, "You are dilated one centimeter." Neither of these is wanted which is why your doctor needs to know if you think you are having contractions. Higher-order multiple pregnancies make it especially difficult to differentiate between contractions causing preterm labor and contractions that are not. Since it is difficult to tell if you are in preterm labor, always contact your doctor if you have any questions or concerns.

Why is it important? Preterm labor resulting in delivery is the most significant major complication of higher-order multiple pregnancies. Almost all triplets (between 75 and 100%) or more are born prematurely. The earlier the babies are born the more likely there will be lifelong challenges. Having babies in the NICU is very emotional for families, especially the not knowing from day-to-day how the babies will do. Having one baby come home but others still hospitalized is difficult. Parents often have financial concerns too. The average hospital costs for a multiple birth in the US can be considerably higher than that of an uncomplicated single birth. In fact, the hospital cost of a triplet delivery is often 10 to 20 times higher than that of a single birth. The primary reason the costs are so much higher for twins, and especially triplets or more is neonatal care for babies delivered prematurely. Every week a pregnancy involving multiples can be extended closer to term saves not only a significant amount of money in initial hospital costs, but also goes a long way toward a healthier outcome for your babies reducing lifetime medical costs as well.

Signs and Symptoms of Preterm Labor

Contracting during any pregnancy is 100% normal and to be expected. A woman's uterus contracts at different times throughout the entire pregnancy; however, most women are not able to feel it until after 18- 20 weeks. You might notice a tightening in your abdomen when you move from a sitting to a standing position, when getting out of bed in the morning or when getting up off the toilet. That is normal. The challenge is trying to learn the difference between normal contractions and contractions that could mean something more.

Preterm labor can have various warning signs. You do not need to have all of them to be in preterm labor; you may only have one or two symptoms. If you develop any of the following symptoms, call your doctor so he/she can evaluate the need for treatment:

- **Uterine contractions**: Even if you had a prior full-term pregnancy with labor, you may or may not feel or recognize uterine contractions. You can use your fingertips to feel a hardening or tightening of your abdomen. (See section in this chapter on self-palpation for contractions for more detailed information.)

- **Menstrual type cramps**: Cramps are usually felt low and can be either constant or rhythmic.

- **Backache**: Pain in the lower back that may radiate to the front and is not relieved with a change in position.

- **Intestinal cramps**: Pains similar to "gas pains."

- **Pressure in the pelvis**: Pain in the lower abdominal or radiating down to the legs.

- **Increase or change in vaginal discharge**.

- **A general feeling that something is not right**.

Unfortunately, sometimes there are no signs or symptoms that you can detect.

Preterm Labor: What You Can Do

Preterm labor may be an expected complication of a multiple pregnancy and some expectant mothers think, "If I am going to have preterm labor anyway, it does not matter what I do or not do. Why not live it up until labor starts?" This is definitely NOT the best approach. Mothers can certainly help delay probable preterm labor with good prenatal care, eating a well-balanced diet, getting plenty of rest and monitoring their bodies for signs of preterm labor. In addition, the timely treatment of preterm labor increases the chances of prolonging the pregnancy until the infants have the best opportunity for a positive outcome.

Contractions are normal and healthy in all pregnancies. In higher-order multiple pregnancies you just generally do not feel them all. Learning what is normal for you (for example, usually 0-4 contractions per hour) is important. Many pregnant mothers of multiples start to have contractions they can identify by tightening or palpation around 16 weeks. Two of the most important steps you can take to help prevent preterm labor are hydration (drinking plenty of fluids) and self-palpation for contractions (described in more detail later in this chapter). Below is a list of other ways you can help prevent preterm labor.

Steps to Help Prevent Preterm Labor

1. Get early and regular prenatal care as soon as you know you are expecting.

2. Stay hydrated.

3. Become aware of the signals your body gives you, including info from self-palpating for contractions.

4. Learn the steps you can take to ease preterm labor symptoms should they occur. [See list in this section.]

5. Understand which activities might be contributing to the symptoms of preterm labor or increased contractions such as walking, sitting, working or just too much activity.

6. Consider ways to change your daily activities to reduce or avoid preterm labor.

7. Avoid constipation.

Steps to Take When Experiencing Symptoms of Preterm Labor

1. Stop what you are doing.

2. Drink 2-3 glasses of water or juice.

3. Lie down on your left side for one hour. You may want to use a straw to drink while lying down.

4. Call your health care provider or go to the hospital if the symptoms get worse during that one hour.

5. Return to light activity only if the symptoms go away after the hour, but do not go back to what you were doing when the symptoms began.

6. If the symptoms return after an hour of rest, call your health care provider right away. Never ignore preterm labor symptoms or assume they are not important.

7. Be sure to tell your provider at your next prenatal visit what symptoms you experienced and what you did about them.

Self-Palpation for Contractions

This technique can help you learn when contractions occur. You will want to try this because some women, even if they have had a previous full-term pregnancy, cannot feel their contractions very well. Start this technique between week 16 and week 20. You will need to put aside an hour in the morning and an hour in the evening to do a self-check. You will need a piece of paper, pen/pencil and a watch or clock with a second hand. With these items lie comfortably on your left side using pillows for support (try not to fall asleep) or just put your feet up; whatever is most comfortable for you. Using your fingertips, gently feel the top of the uterus. Place your hands on either side of your abdomen with your fingers fanned. Your pinky should point between your hips and pubic bone and your thumb up toward your rib cage. Keep your hands here for the entire hour. If you feel a tightening on both sides at the same time that is most likely a contraction. If the tightening is just on one side, then it is most likely gas or another muscle contracting. At some point during your pregnancy your belly may feel as hard as a rock ALL of the time, and if you do not take the time to monitor yourself before that point, there is a good chance you will not know you are contracting later.

When the uterus is relaxed it will feel soft; however, a contraction will cause the uterus to become firm and hard and will affect the entire muscle top to bottom. When a contraction is felt, check the clock and count how long it takes the uterus to become soft again; write down the length of time. Also, write down the time between contractions and any symptoms, recent activity level, medications or other relevant information. If you have more than three contractions per hour or less than 15 minutes between any contractions, you should assume you are experiencing preterm labor, so call your physician unless directed otherwise. Some women have difficulty doing self-palpation whether or not they had a previous pregnancy.

The week after you start monitoring yourself ask your doctor if it would be possible for you to come in for your next visit an hour early or if you could stay an hour after to use the monitor in his office to make sure you are actually picking up the contractions correctly. If possible have someone else accompany you on this visit and ask them to watch the monitor or have it facing away from you. The monitor will identify a contraction before you are able to feel it much like you see the lightning before you hear the thunder. Ask whoever is with you not to say anything until the contraction has passed so he/she does not give you that information. Ideally you will learn to identify tightening on your own. If after an hour you are not confident you are picking up all of your contractions, ask if you can repeat this at your next visit.

Diagnosing and Treating Preterm Labor

If you are diagnosed with preterm labor your physician may use medications called tocolytics and bedrest to delay delivery. Some doctors will only delay delivery 24 hours until steroids, given to mature the babies' lungs, have taken effect. Others will use tocolytics to delay birth for weeks or even months.

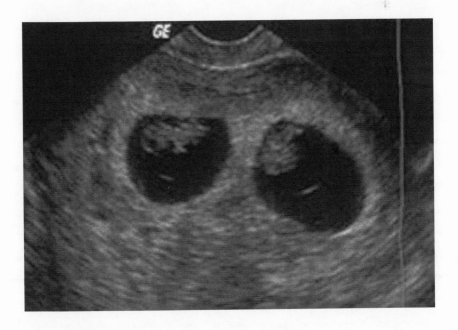

Fetal Fibronectin

Although this test does not diagnose preterm labor it does provide the physician an idea if you are likely to have labor within the next two weeks. The Fetal Fibronectin (fFN) test checks vaginal secretions for the presence of fFN. Fetal fibronectin is a protein that acts as a "glue" to bind the amniotic membranes to the wall of the uterus. This test is performed much like a pap smear and is used to identify the risk of premature delivery. The test is typically performed between 22-34 weeks gestation and may be repeated every 2 weeks.

The results are usually complete within 24 hours, and the rapid test can provide results within one hour. Results are said to be "positive" or "negative." A positive test result usually occurs when spontaneous labor is likely to occur within the next 2-3 weeks. A positive fFN test prior to 37 weeks gestation indicates the patient is at risk for preterm delivery. The average time from a positive fFn test until delivery is 17 days in multiple gestations.

A negative test means the mother is unlikely to deliver within the next 7-14 days. However, in a higher-order multiple pregnancy a negative test result is not as predictive of preterm labor as in singleton pregnancies.

Home Uterine Activity Monitoring

Home Uterine Activity Monitoring (HUAM) detects and records uterine contractions that a woman pregnant with multiples may not feel. It involves the use of a band that is worn around the abdomen and a small unit that houses the electronics. Monitoring is done 2 times a day for 1 hour each. The mother has a button to push whenever she feels a contraction. The data is then downloaded and transmitted via the phone to a nurse who analyzes the information. The nurse has standing orders, based on the number of contractions, for what he or she instructs the patient to do. The mother may be instructed to drink water, lie on her left side and retest or if the mother is on a tocolytic, she may be instructed to take an extra dose. The nurse then notifies the physician if needed. This contact with a nurse is very beneficial in high-risk pregnancies; some physicians believe it is as or more beneficial than the device.

HUAM is used to detect contractions, but it does not diagnose preterm labor directly. The physician takes the information from the monitoring session and uses it to make a diagnosis and prescribe treatment. The American College of Obstetricians and Gynecologists (ACOG) takes the position that HUAM does not "prevent preterm birth" and therefore many physicians do not use it, and insurance companies may not want to cover it. On the other hand, many higher-order multiple mothers feel HUAM saved their babies' lives by immediately alerting them when preterm labor had started allowing them to receive appropriate treatment. Although many doctors agree that HUAM does not prevent preterm birth, the device can let them know there is an increase in uterine irritability or contractions. This could be preterm labor and the mother may need immediate medical attention.

HUAM can and should be used as a teaching device. Mothers can practice self-palpation at the same time as they are utilizing HUAM, and the nurse can teach the mother how to "mark" the monitor when she feels something that may be a contraction. This approach saves money by avoiding hospitalization allowing the mother to stay at home longer. It also allows the mother to determine whether she is feeling an actual contraction so she can monitor her activity level to make sure she is not doing too much. Finally, it allows her to feel as if she has a little more control over her pregnancy.

Tocolytics

Earlier in this book you read that almost all HOM and many twin pregnancies have preterm labor concerns. In HOM pregnancies preterm labor begins earlier than in singleton and typical twin pregnancies. Therefore, many doctors will use medications to help control preterm labor and allow the babies more time to grow in the womb before birth. These medications are called tocolytics and are used to decrease the strength and number of contractions that can cause the cervix to dilate. Using different mechanisms, these medications relax smooth muscles like those in the uterus. Each of these medications, while safe to use, can have side effects that are usually not severe. Your doctor should explain the medications used and their side effects prior to its use. Once on the medication, be sure to speak with your doctor about what may occur with whichever medication he may prescribe. Let your doctor know about any side affects you notice. Some doctors only use tocolytics for a short period of time (48 hours) at low doses to allow steroids to enhance fetal lung development; however, some physicians have had success treating preterm labor in higher-order pregnancies using tocolytics for weeks or even months, at times with higher doses than used with a singleton pregnancy. Doctors generally prescribe one or more of the tocolytics that we discuss in this section.

Terbutaline - Terbutaline Sulfate, also known as terbutaline or Brethine, is a bronchodilator that decreases airway resistance in the lungs. It also affects the smooth muscle of the uterus to decrease contractions. Terbutaline acts on cells in the body in a fashion similar to epinephrine (adrenaline) and can currently be given subcutaneously (by injection). If you speak with mothers who have delivered prior to February 2011, they may mention taking terbutaline by mouth or using a pump (commonly known as a T-pump). In February 2011, the US Food and Drug Administration (FDA) issued a Drug Safety Communication that questioned the safety and effectiveness of oral terbutaline and terbutaline given by a pump. There continues to be discussion regarding the use of terbutaline in oral and pump forms. However, currently terbutaline can be used only subcutaneously in a hospital setting generally for short-term use to stop contractions.

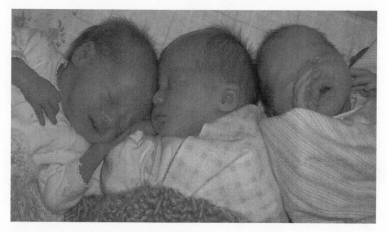

Some potential side effects include:

- Nervousness or feeling jittery
- Breathlessness and /or increased heart rate
- Headaches
- Increase in blood sugar levels

Indomethacin - Indomethacin, also called Indocin, is classified as a non-steroidal medication. Aspirin is also a drug in this category. Indocin works as an anti-inflammatory, fever reducer and analgesic (pain relieving) drug. It also relaxes the muscle of the uterus. Indocin is a very effective medication, given orally or by suppository, but can only be given for 24-72 hours due to side effects. The concern is that with extended use it can cause stomach ulcers in a baby and increases the chance of the babies developing necrotizing enterocolitis (NEC- a complication of prematurity that may cause areas of the intestine to die). For higher-order multiple pregnancies, Indocin can be used prior to 32 weeks gestation.

Two other non-steroidal drugs that can be used to decrease contractions are toradol and ibuprofen. Toradol can be given intravenously (IV) or intramuscularly (injection into the muscle) in the hospital. Ibuprofen (brand name Motrin) can be used orally (600 mg every 6 hours) either in the hospital or home.

A possible side effect of the non-steroidal medications is a possible decrease in the amniotic fluid volume. This may or may not be a wanted side effect. These medications should be stopped at about 32 weeks gestation due to a small chance that the ductus arteriosus (a small connection in the heart) will close too soon. Possible side effects to the mother may include:

- Nausea and vomiting
- Abdominal pain
- Depression
- Dizziness

Procardia - Procardia, also known as Nifedipine or Adalat, is classified as a calcium antagonist or calcium channel blocker. It affects the calcium channels in the individual muscle cells by acting like plugs in drains to prevent contractions. Procardia does not affect the calcium used in building bones and is frequently used for heart problems because it slows heart rate and reduces blood pressure. It can be used for extended treatment to decrease contractions and treat preterm labor. Possible side effects to the expectant mother may include:

- Headache
- Facial flushing
- Lightheadedness
- Nausea
- Heart palpitations

Magnesium Sulfate - Treatment with magnesium sulfate, also known as mag, is a more aggressive treatment for preterm labor. This medication requires hospitalization and is administered intravenously (IV). There are perinatologists that utilize mag at high doses and for weeks (even months) if necessary to obtain a longer gestation for the babies. One of these is Dr. John Elliott who shared his treatment perspective in chapter 3. As noted by Dr. Elliott:

"For HOM pregnancies, a higher dose of mag is sometimes needed and for a longer time. To control preterm labor and prevent an early birth, I will prescribe an initial dose of 6 grams followed by 3-5 grams per hour. This may take days to bring PTL under control in the HOM pregnancy. After acute PTL has stopped I will continue to utilize mag for weeks or even months to obtain older gestational ages at birth if necessary."

During treatment with magnesium sulfate, blood levels are checked to determine the proper dosage for each situation. Hospitals need to employ rigid protocols and safety checks when administering magnesium sulfate such as double-checking the initial loading dose with two RN's and frequent checking of the patient by nursing staff to watch reflexes, breathing and the oxygen and/or heart monitor. During treatment the mother will need to record her fluid intake and nurses should check urine output. Side effects usually go away within a few days and are worse with the initial loading dose. These possible side effects usually can be tolerated to obtain a longer gestation for your babies.

- Feeling flushed and warm
- Increased perspiration
- Nystagmus (involuntary twitching of eyeball)
- Nausea and vomiting
- Blurred vision and slurred speech
- Light-headedness or headache
- Lethargy and sluggishness
- Nasal stuffiness
- Diarrhea or constipation
- Feeling foggy or like having a really bad flu
- A metallic taste in the mouth (like sucking on a copper penny)

- Slow breathing
- Slow reflexes
- Chest pain especially if on another tocolytic
- A small increased risk of pulmonary edema in multiple gestations
- Decreased fetal heart rate
- Drowsy newborn
- Babies with a weak cry or sucking reflex

Many mothers have found the following coping mechanisms helpful during treatment with magnesium sulfate:

- Wearing light weight clothing
- Having a fan blowing near the face
- Limiting visitors
- Having a spouse or other adult present when the physician visits

Although each of these medications may have some unpleasant side effects, it is important to note that your doctor will only incorporate them into your pregnancy management plan if he believes it is absolutely necessary. Your goal is to deliver your babies at the latest gestational age possible. With the use of these medications, even with side effects, many women have been able to deliver their babies at a later gestational age.

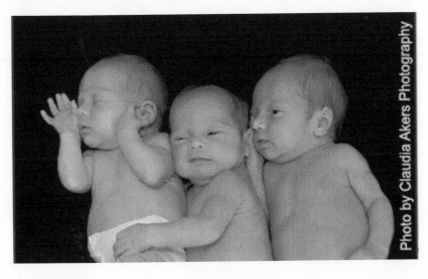

Photo by Claudia Akers Photography

Bedrest

"Last year at this time I was out of work on disability with my pregnancy. I understand how reluctant/frustrated you might be feeling, but by the last day of work (I was a 1ˢᵗ grade teacher) I was SO ready to rest!"

"Some doctors have set protocols for bedrest but that does not necessarily mean it will not start earlier or later. You will need to completely understand what is meant by the term "bedrest." Can you go up/down stairs? Do you need to lie down only? Can you sit up in recliner or go to doctor appointments? Are you allowed to get up at all? My doctor recommended bedrest at 18 weeks gestation. It seems like more mothers are put on bedrest than not, but bedrest can be different for everyone."

Bedrest Activity Level and Bedrest Activity Checklist

Bedrest can mean various levels of activity to different doctors and between you and your doctor. To help you know what level of bedrest your doctor wants you to follow, you can use the Bedrest Activity Checklist below. [The checklist is also included in the Welcome Basket when you join MOST.] We encourage you to use this list to clarify with your health care provider what you are allowed to do and in what amount.

Bedrest Activity Checklist

(Discuss with your physician the appropriate level of activity for each stage of your pregnancy)

Overall Activity Level:

___ Normal

___ Slight Decrease

___ Significant Decrease

___ Complete Bedrest

Mobility:

(Your doctor should know if you live in a multi-story house or walk up several flights of stairs to your apartment.):

___ Normal mobility

___ Limited (sitting mostly)

___ Lie down ____ hours per day

___ May go up/down stairs ___ times

___ Light walking only

___ Sit to eat only

___ Recline all day

___ Lie flat all day (on left or right side?)

___ Use wheelchair

Employment

(Your physician should know what your job entails: physical requirements like how much time you spend standing, stress level, details of your commute, etc.):

___ Work full-time as usual

___ Work part-time for only _____ hours

___ Work from home for only _____ hours

    In what position: ____ chair

                       ____ recliner

                       ____ lying on side

___ Other _____

___ Stop working completely

Childcare for Siblings:

___ Care for children as usual

___ No breastfeeding

___ No carrying children

___ No lifting children

___ No bending or stooping

___ Need childcare provider

Leisure Activities:

___ Normal activities

___ Stop intense activities like jogging, climbing, etc.

___ Short walks only

___ Sit at desk/table only

___ Recline: watch TV, talk on phone, read

___ Activities lying down only

Driving:

___ Drive as normal

___ Drive only as needed

___ Passenger only

___ Ride only to appointments

Household Activities:

___ Heavy: laundry, vacuum, change bed sheets

___ Prepare meals, wash dishes (standing)

___ Light: dusting, straighten beds

___ Grocery shopping

___ Other _____

Sexual Relations:

___ Normal relations

___ Occasional relations only

___ Avoid intercourse

___ Avoid female stimulation/orgasm

___ No sexual relations

Bathroom Privileges:

___ Normal bathroom privileges

___ Avoid constipation

___ Must use bedside toilet

___ Must use bedpan

____ Short showers only

____ Shower only (Sitting down using shower chair)

____ Bath in a tub only (In a reclined position)

____ Bedside sponge bath only

____ Other _____

Bedrest is recommended for various reasons and for various lengths of time. Sometimes your doctor will want you to stay off your feet for a few days after a procedure early in your pregnancy or if you are experiencing vaginal bleeding. Some mothers are put on strict bedrest for months at a time. Many mothers restrict their own activities because they feel that their body needs to take it easy. Some women adjust easily to bedrest while others find it more difficult. Remembering that you are doing this for your babies usually makes bedrest easier. It really is for only a short time even though some days might feel like forever!

Tips for Managing Bedrest

Bedrest sounds so much easier than it actually is: physically, mentally and emotionally. The following are many of the different emotions expectant mothers have described feeling while on bedrest:

- A loss of independence as a result of a reduction in activity level, inability to care for family and perhaps even total dependence on others

- Feelings of inadequacy because you are not able to have a "normal" pregnancy like other women, are not able to work outside the home or care for other children and your household.

- Feelings of helplessness/loss of control may be experienced by both parents due to an inability to change the situation. Partners may feel overburdened by an increased workload at home or financial burdens.

- Feelings of isolation or being different from others having "normal" pregnancies and being confined to home, bed or the hospital. Support systems normally available through work or outside activities may be gone due to activity restrictions or hospital isolation. You may be worried about your health and the well-being of your unborn children.

- Feeling misunderstood when others say you are lucky to get to "rest" and "lie around all day" when bedrest and gestating is actually the expectant mothers "work" right now and must be taken seriously. Some of the medications and treatments are also not much fun.

- The major shift in household responsibilities means the entire burden of the household is now on the co-parent or is a huge concern for a single mother or one with a partner not able or willing to help.

- Frustration caused by watching other parents excitedly prepare for their baby's birth and not being able to do this. Expectant parents of multiples may be unable to make decisions or preparations due to uncertainty of the outcome especially if they have had past pregnancy losses. Sometimes people try to help by saying "everything will be all right" but parents know this is not always the case.

- The financial demands of going from a double to a single income when medical bills are rising especially when the mother may have carried the insurance or been a major financial contributor.

Expectant mothers have found online support groups to be a place to share anxieties during this time. Be careful of sharing information and remember that not all sites have accurate medical information. Other ways to decrease stress during bedrest include practicing relaxation techniques, having someone who can listen, and knowing that someone else is in a similar situation. Contact MOST to get in touch with other mothers in similar circumstances or have been in those circumstances.

Bedrest might be recommended while you are at home or you might be admitted to the hospital for bedrest. Here are 20 tips and ideas from Sidelines of Oregon to help you manage bedrest.

1. Wear clothes during the day if possible and be neat and clean: keep up personal hygiene

2. Set goals, keep them in mind and focus on WHY you are doing this not WHAT you are doing

3. Shop by phone or online

4. Plan your weekly meal menus and organize the grocery list.

5. Consider using a grocery delivery services from your local store or online

6. Do crossword, word-search or jigsaw puzzles

7. Have visitors but only when you feel up to it. Watch favorite shows together

8. Do something special for yourself such as having someone come in to give a manicure, pedicure or facial

9. Keep a journal of your pregnancy and a calendar to chart your progress.

10. Focus on how far you have come, not how far you have to go

11. Listen to books on tape or learn a new language with tapes from the library

12. Make a list of tasks people can do for you, so when they ask, you can easily offer them a choice.

13. Request a childbirth class in the home if available

14. Have a "date" with your partner with take-out food and candles

15. Do craft projects such as cross stitch, needlepoint, knitting, etc. to make something special for the babies or someone else

16. Do passive bedrest exercises with approval from your physician.

17. Read books on high-risk pregnancy, multiples, and premature babies such as this one

18. Pay bills, compile tax data, reorganize files or update your address book

19. Order and address birth announcements

20. Call a friend, relative or support person, such as someone from MOST or a local support volunteer, each day. Find someone who understands your fears and hopes.

You also may want to use this time to consider pediatricians. While direct experience caring for multiples may be helpful, a more important consideration is whether the pediatrician has experience caring for children born preterm or who may face developmental delays because of a preterm birth. Consider the location of the office as well as the parking, Can you safely load and unload all the babies? Will the office schedule all the children for the same visit? See the resources at the end of this chapter for articles that have more advice on factors to consider when picking a pediatrician.

Older Children and Bedrest

If you have older children, finding someone else to care for them during bedrest may be easier on you. Whether or not that is possible, below are some ideas to entertain them. This can be challenging, but try to make the best of the situation.

The days/weeks/months you are on bedrest are really just a short period of time in your children's lives, and in the long run delivering the healthiest babies possible is better for the babies, their older siblings and for you:

- If you have toddlers and no older children, make your bedroom into a giant playpen. Put everything out of reach and shut the door so you do not have to worry about where your child is.
- Watch television, read, play board or video games or just talk
- Make videos together of you and your child(ren) singing or talking
- Have a small ice chest next to your bed packed with the day's drinks and snacks. Keep supplies/toys in a laundry basket near your bed.
- Make a paper chain and have your child take one off for every day
- Keep a roll of paper towels near your bed for spills
- Use an old sheet or blanket as a playtime cover to spare your bedspread
- Let your child play under the covers or Play "I Spy"
- Play "bed-bowling" with paper cups and a small ball
- Play "bed-basketball" by tossing rolled up socks into an empty basket
- Play "bedspread traffic" using small cars to follow the bedspread design
- Go bed fishing using magnets and paper fish with paper clips
- Use a mirror to make faces expressing feelings
- Make hand shadows on the wall with a flashlight.
- Work jigsaw puzzles, construct building blocks or play board games
- Play red light-green light with you being the traffic cop
- Cut up magazines and paste them on cardboard for paper dolls
- Get children's books from the library and read
- Use coloring books or play dough
- Trace letters/numbers on your child's back that they can guess

Fetal Movement Monitoring

Using a technique similar to the one learned earlier in your pregnancy to track contractions, you can also track fetal movements later in your pregnancy to help you become more aware of your babies. Starting at about 28 weeks gestation, simply note on paper how many movements each baby has within an hour. Whether you are actually on bedrest or not, fetal movement monitoring is important because sometimes a decrease in a baby's movement can indicate a problem. The earlier you become aware of a change in fetal movement patterns, the better chance your physician has of addressing potential complications.

Fetal movement monitoring, also sometimes referred to as kick counting, is done once or twice a day when the babies are most active. Performing the test twice a day, once in the morning and once in the evening, is ideal. To perform the test, get a notebook and pen and then get comfortable, usually by lying on your left side in bed. Place your hands on each side of your belly for 1 hour. Note on your paper how many movements you feel for each baby. You may not be 100% accurate about which baby is kicking at any given moment but should try your best to identify each baby. Try to count the movements of each baby and write that down. Typically, you will have some idea where each baby is located in the uterus at this point in the pregnancy and can distinguish between each of the babies' movements most of the time. At first you will just be determining what is typical for each baby. Once a baseline is set, if a baby does not seem to be moving as much as normal, you may want to retest. If there are significant changes or should you feel concerned, you should let your physician know. The written log will likely prove very helpful in explaining your concerns.

Long-Term Hospitalization Prior to Delivery

You might need to be hospitalized for any number of reasons including preterm labor. Some women find knowing that they and their babies are well cared for in the hospital reassuring. Other women are anxious about being hospitalized. Realize that if your doctor admits you to the hospital, he feels that the hospital is the best place for you and your babies to be at this time.

If you need to go to the hospital, you may be directed to the Emergency Department (ED). Most EDs will send an expectant mother experiencing complications directly to Labor and Delivery rather than treating her in the ED. Once in the Labor and Delivery unit you will be placed on a fetal monitor to detect uterine contractions and monitor the babies' heartbeats. Some doctors will not order continuous monitoring of the babies' heartbeats but do only occasional checks. The nurse will ask you many questions and may run one or more tests including:

- Blood count
- Urinalysis
- Fetal Fibronectin test (see details earlier in this chapter)
- Ultrasound
- Cervical exam (if possible, have done by **your** physician)

If preterm labor is diagnosed, the doctor must determine whether stopping labor is safe. For example, if the mother has a uterine infection, prolonging the pregnancy may not be safe. Other factors used to assess the safety of prolonging a pregnancy include the health of the babies and mother. Your doctor should discuss all the alternatives with you and together determine the proper course of treatment. As we wrote earlier, discussing how early in your pregnancy your doctor is willing to be proactive in stopping contractions is important. Some doctors will not treat preterm labor or contractions before 24 weeks gestation.

Items You May Wish to Have With You at the Hospital

- Hair bands or clips to pull back hair (especially if you plan on pumping or breastfeeding after delivery)

151

- A calendar (paper copy, laptop or phone).You can use this to schedule offers of help after the babies come home or to care for older children

- Ear plugs or an MP3 player to block out hospital noises

- Lip balm and skin cream as hospital air is quite dry

- Your own robe and slippers

- High-waisted underwear to avoid rubbing the incision after delivery

- Your own sanitary pads

- A nursing bra and pads if you plan to breastfeed or pump (do not buy many bras ahead of time as you may not know what size you will be wearing)

- A special pillow, blanket or other comfort and mementos of home

- Camera or video camera to record the pregnancy if desired

- A contact list or electronic directory to contact friends and family members (If you have Internet access, you can set up a personal blog or MOST CarePage at www.MOSTonline.org/CarePages)

- A disposable camera for each baby's NICU isolette labeled with your name and phone

- If able to store and keep safe, your laptop or smart phone. Remember to bring the chargers!

Tips to Prepare Children for Mother's Hospitalization

There are several ways to help prepare other children for your hospitalization. Some children will go with the flow while others have a hard time. Many children take their cues from you and other family members. If you are relaxed and take it in stride, they are more likely to as well. Of course, sometimes it does not make a difference. Just remember you are doing this for your older children too by giving them the healthiest siblings possible. Knowing your other children are cared for can help decrease the stress of being hospitalized. Here are a few things you can do to make your hospitalization easier on them.

- Have two copies of favorite books available: one for home and one for the hospital to read together each night over the phone or when he or she visits. This can help keep your child's bedtime routine familiar.

- Update and read with older siblings' their baby books or recall the story of their births. If you have already purchased baby books for your multiples, you can start filling those in together with such information as your family tree.

- Sing songs together, and maybe even record them so they can be played while you are away. Include in the recording a reading of some of their favorite books, stories of special memories you have shared and the story of their birth.

- Arrange to buy clothing or school supplies in advance depending on your due date.

- Watch age-appropriate movies featuring multiples such as *Huey, Dewy and Louie.*

- If possible, establish a routine for you children to visit on a regular basis such as every Friday at 6 pm for dinner.

- As much as possible have caretakers keep a routine at home for school, meals, naps, extra-curricular activities, baths, bedtime, etc.

- Discover age-appropriate books to read with the older siblings to help provide information about life with triplets such as:

  o *Thumper's Little Sisters* (a Disney book)
  o *Babar the Elephant or Peter Rabbit*
  o Maj Lindman series (numerous books in each series)
  o *Flicka, Ricka and Dicka* three Swedish girls
  o *Snipp, Snapp and Snurr* three little boys
  o *Triplets* by Felix Pirani (a book about triplet girls)

Resources

Preterm Labor

- National Institute of Child Health and Human Development: www.nichd.nih.gov/health/topics/Preterm_Labor_and_Birth.cfm

- American College of Obstetrics and Gynecology: www.acog.org/~/media/For%20Patients/faq087.pdf

Tocolytic Medication

- See a list of journal publication citations on tocolytics by Dr Elliott and others in the field of perinatology at the end of the section titled "A Perinatologist's Perspective on Managing Higher-Order Multiple Pregnancies" of Chapter 3 in this book.

Bedrest

- Sidelines is a national, non-profit organization founded in 1991 by two mothers who experienced bedrest personally and wanted to support other high-risk mothers and their families. The website contains tips for women on surviving bedrest: www.sidelines.org, (888) 447-4754 (HI-RISK4), or sidelines@sidelines.org

- CarePages are private personalized web pages that help families receive support from friends and family, update family and friends on their progress and keep in touch with their support network before, during and after hospitalization or bedrest www.MOSTonline.org/CarePages/

- Bedrest information and support: http://fpb.cwru.edu/Bedrest/

- Compliance Assistance for the Family and Medical Leave Act (FMLA): www.dol.gov/whd/regs/compliance/ca_main.htm

- Patient Advocate Foundation is a national non-profit organization that seeks to safeguard patients through effective mediation assuring access to care, maintenance of employment and preservation of their financial stability: www.patientadvocate.org/

- Bedrest Activity Checklist Download:
  www.mostonline.org/sunshop/dd/BedrestChecklistBookmark2.pdf

- *Pregnancy Bedrest* by Judy Maloni, RN, PhD, FAAN

- *Pregnancy Bedrest: A Journey of Love* by Wanda Hale

Choosing a Pediatrician

- Info and questions to consider: *Should I choose **a pediatrician who specializes in multiples?*** http://www.mostonline.org/faq36.htm

- Article on the MOST blog: *How To Find and Interview A Pediatrician*
  http://www.mostonline.org/wordpress/?p=4630

- Article from the MOST Library: *What is a developmental pediatrician?*
  http://www.mostonline.org/sunshop/index.php?l=product_detail&p=46

Chapter 7: Preparing Yourself, Family and Home

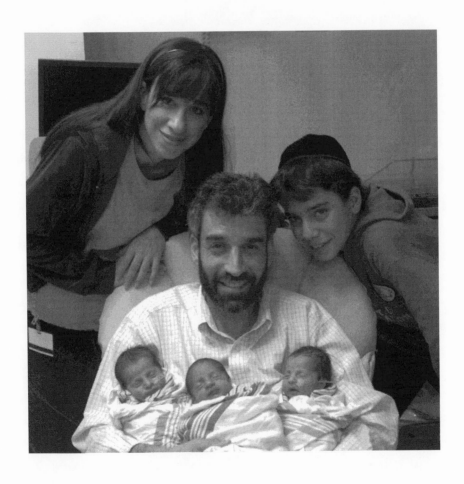

"Before our babies were born, I never thought about considering live-in help. We could not afford it even if I had. After the babies came home from the hospital, we managed on our own until my husband had to return to work. We were fortunate that our church sent some senior citizens to volunteer for 4 hours a day. They were wonderful! Soon after, friends with grown children came by to help out several times a week during dinnertime, which also was wonderful. I also had a list of friends who had offered to volunteer as needed. For example if one of the babies was ill or we were just having a VERY rough day, I would call them and they would be here at a moment's notice. (Life savers!) Not until the babies were about 18 months old did we hire a mother's helper for 3 times a week to help when running errands or during baths and dinnertime."

Y ou may need or want to start preparing yourself, your family and your home for your new babies. Here are some suggestions, tips and recommendations to make these preparations as smooth as possible.

Preparing Yourself

Arranging Help

Having help, whether while you are on bedrest or when the babies arrive home, can be very beneficial at least initially. When financially possible or logistically feasible, you should consider using volunteers or paid help in the first few months of the multiples' homecoming. This allows you to rest more and provides more hands-on help for the infants. Some mothers have a strong sense of privacy and do not want others to come into the home. Others are open to the idea of help. You may not need or want help 24 hours a day, or you may have family members or friends who are willing to assist you during the day and/or night. Some families received help from a religious or civic group, but for many families, outside help was not available and still they were very successful managing on their own. Whatever you decide be sure to consider your needs and the babies' needs.

Naming the Babies

Like the process of naming any newborn, new parents should consider how the baby's first name fits with the baby's last name. For example if your last name is Bond, do you really want to name your son James, or if your last name is Showers do you want to name your daughter April?

Sometimes parents choose rhyming names or names that start with the same first letter. Although this approach acknowledges the closeness of your babies, these names can also cause some confusion as the children grow. Insurance companies sometimes have trouble processing claims when several babies who are born on the same day have the same first initial and last name. Some families have also reported conflicts with Social Security Administration, so naming can be an important consideration. Although naming your children is a very personal decision, giving each child his or her own distinct first name sets the stage for him or her to be treated as an individual and not only as part of a unit or group.

Preparing to Breastfeed

"Breast milk is definitely easier for babies to digest plus all the added benefits it gives their immune systems. My girls started receiving my breast milk through tube feedings the first couple of days and then began to learn how to drink from a bottle of pumped breast milk. They came home after 2 weeks but never really caught on to actually nursing, so I pumped for 4 months. It was tiresome, and I felt like I was permanently connected to the pump, but I think I would have felt the same way nursing. I would have spent most of my time feeding either way."

If you decide to breastfeed your multiples, the first step is to secure support for your decision. Maybe you are unsure but want to try breastfeeding. Inform your spouse or other support person and notify your health care professionals as soon as possible. If your pediatrician does not know about breastfeeding multiples or that many mothers of triplets and quadruplets have been successful breastfeeding, you can still find information and support. Other steps you can take to prepare include:

- **Attending a class:** Many hospitals host breastfeeding classes for expectant mothers of multiples. If not, attend the regular breastfeeding classes if possible, but be sure to sign up and attend this early during pregnancy, ideally before 20 weeks, just in case your pregnancy requires an extended period of bedrest or limited activity. If you are hospitalized prior to delivery, you can request to meet with the Lactation Consultant or nurse educator at your bedside.

- **Attending a La Leche League meeting:** There you can see mothers nursing and talk to a leader. If the leader has not had experience with mothers who have breastfed multiples, she should be able to refer you to another leader.

- **Asking what breastfeeding options are available at the hospital:** Do they offer pumping stations, milk storage, and pump supplies at the NICU, postpartum unit, and/or nursery? You may also want to ask about the hospital policy and procedure for bringing breast milk to the babies. The hospital lactation consultant can help you locate companies that rent or sell quality (hospital grade) breast pumps. You can have the breast pump on hand even before you deliver. Pregnancy bedrest is a good time to find out how to rent a quality electric breast pump and if insurance will cover it since your babies will be preterm. Many families who put this off until the mother's discharge find themselves scrambling for a pump, bottles, labels and sterile supplies.

- **Meeting the professionals:** Schedule a tour of the NICU around 26 weeks gestation or even earlier. While on the tour meet the nurse in charge, Lactation Consultant and the social worker if possible. Find out about parent procedures and protocol. Many expectant/new parents find the NICU overwhelming and scary at first, but the more they understand and are familiar with the unit, the less anxiety provoking it will be. For example, a nurse or the lactation specialist can show you how to assemble and position the pump correctly. You should gather the contact information for these individuals and be sure to ask the lactation consultant if she could put you in touch with other mothers of premature multiples who successfully used the pump and/or nursed at the breast after the babies were discharged.

- **Talking to several women:** Everyone's situation and personalities are different, so try to talk with several women keeping an open mind to learn from them. MOST has a wonderful Breastfeeding booklet that you can order as well as several FAQs on breastfeeding available on the MOST website. [See Resources at the end of this chapter.]

- **Avoiding these activities**: Some pregnancy books still suggest a woman 'toughen' her nipples prior during pregnancy by rubbing them with a terry cloth towel after showering. This activity is **NOT recommended** for any pregnancy and especially not a high-risk pregnancy. A mother expecting multiples should NEVER toughen her nipples as nipple stimulation can trigger preterm labor. Mothers experiencing a high-risk pregnancy also should not practice using a breast pump on her breasts while it is turned on before delivery because it could cause contractions or preterm labor.

Photo by Lifetouch Portrait Studios

Journaling

As discussed earlier, writing your thoughts, fears and dreams can help you prepare for the changes in your life that are occurring now and will occur after delivery. Whether kept in the same notebook as your medical notes or in a separate journal, this will be a keepsake in the years to come. Some women like to journal online on a blog or personal web page. If you do journal online, remember that this information is available to just about anyone and will be available for decades to come. [See Chapter 9 "Online safety and security for your family" for more information about online writing.]

Questions about Personal Concerns and Care

Other concerns and questions mothers have had in the past are listed below along with a few of their coping tips. Note that these are designed to be general coping tips, and again, be sure to keep your doctor and nurses informed if you have any unexpected pain or unanswered questions.

When will I feel the babies move?

"I felt like I had aliens inside of me! One foot here, an elbow there, even a behind pushing out - all at the same time."

Usually the first movements felt are a slight tickle inside. Some women describe this as feeling as if they have butterflies inside their belly. If you softly drum your fingertips across your other forearm, this is similar to what it feels like. If you feel this up high near your rib cage, over by your hips or down by your pubic bone it is probably gas, but if you are feeling it toward the center of your abdomen it is most likely one of your precious babies. The earliest these movements are felt is usually around 16 weeks. They are subtle and you have a better chance knowing what those little twitches are if you have been pregnant before. Many women do not feel movement until around 20 weeks gestation.

The evening hours are usually very active for the babies. [See Chapter 6 for information about fetal movement counting.] Having two, three or more babies moving inside of you is one of the greatest possible gifts an expectant mother of multiples can experience. If you were expecting just one baby, you would treasure his movements of course, but feeling movement when pregnant with multiples is so completely different. You learn about their personalities long before they are born. You may have one who is the instigator getting everyone going and then settles down leaving the others to carry on the ruckus. You may have one who is so quiet and seems to sleep a lot or is easily pleased and laid back. You may have one who is squished up around your rib cage and his/her heartbeat cannot be heard by the nurses without hearing yours in the background and vice versa (another special gift). Hopefully you will not have a night owl living with a few morning doves. Feeling each of your babies move is one of the greatest gifts of this pregnancy and so hard to truly explain to someone who has not had multiples.

Yikes, my breasts are tender; what helps?

"Be careful in the shower; do not let the stream of water hit your breasts directly. Ouch! Heat has helped, and I wore a bra 24 hours a day (except when bathing), and that helped a little too. Mine hurt very early on as well but it does get better."

As your breasts get ready to produce milk for the babies you may experience breast tenderness. Wearing a tight fitting bra at all times may help. The size of your breasts will change and you may need a larger band and/or cup size more than once as your pregnancy progresses. Do not spend a lot of money on nursing bras while pregnant because your breasts will most likely increase in size as you produce milk for breastfeeding or pumping after delivery. There are many different styles of bras and a style you did not like for your pre-pregnant body may be the one that fits most comfortably now. A maternity/nursing sleep bra may provide the support you need during the night. Noticing a lump in your breast during pregnancy is not uncommon in any pregnancy, and it is usually a clogged milk duct. Be sure to tell your doctor so it can be evaluated.

What is this pain going down my leg?

"I also had a sciatic nerve pinch and it makes you feel like a million little needles are poking your legs."

- **Sciatic Nerve** - Some women will have mild to severe pain that goes down the leg. This is probably due to the sciatic nerve being pinched by the babies. The sciatic nerve is the largest nerve in the body and it provides sensory and motor function to the legs. If you feel pain that is located on the back of the thigh, the lower part of the leg and/or the sole of the foot your sciatic nerve is probably pinched. You can do a few things to treat the pain. The simplest remedy is to lie on your side, opposite of the pain, to help relieve the pressure on the nerve. If you experience pressure while standing, try elevating one foot and resting it on something. Swimming can ease discomfort if you doctor permits this. A chiropractor may also be helpful. You should not be lifting anything heavier than a ½ gallon of milk or standing for long periods of time, but if you are, it is probably time to stop! You may find that heat or cold applied to the sore area may help. With your doctor's permission, taking acetaminophen may also help to relieve the discomfort.

- **Pubic Bone Separation** - Due to pregnancy hormones the pelvic bone becomes loose in preparation for vaginal childbirth. (Apparently, it did not get the memo that you will most likely be having a C-section.) This may result in pain in the lower back or hips when the pubic bone separation occurs, also called pubic symphysis diastasis. Some women will simply feel pain in the front pubic bone area. The separation usually makes hip or leg movements painful. Always tell your health care provider about this and any other pain or discomfort you may have. Sometimes this type of pain or discomfort is caused by something completely different such as a bladder infection or premature cervical dilation. If the pain is caused by pubic bone separation, many women find that a warm compress being placed over the pubic bone helps. You may want to ask your doctor if you can take some mild pain medication. Some women find they need to use a wheelchair or walker to move around more comfortably. The pain can last a few days or weeks but is usually gone sooner or shortly after delivery.

Will I have stretch marks?

"I did not want stretch marks, but if it meant my babies would be born bigger and healthier because I was bigger, I was all for it! I still have them-I will never wear a bikini again, and I am okay with that."

Most women will get stretch marks due to the large amount of weight gain and skin stretching during their multiple pregnancy. These stretch marks may be on the abdomen, upper thighs and breasts or even around the trunk. There is really nothing that can be used or done to prevent them from forming; however drinking enough fluids and eating healthy will keep your skin in top condition and may lessen the severity. Your genetic background also plays a part in how stretch marks might develop. Skin lotions containing cocoa butter, Shea butter or vitamin E may help your skin feel better, but no lotion or cream has been proven to prevent stretch marks. Just keeping your skin moisturized will help some. Some skin treatments can be done after delivery and breastfeeding/pumping to reduce the marks.

Will a belly binder help?

Some women had good results wearing an abdominal binder while pregnant. A binder it an elastic stretchable band that goes around your lower abdomen. By providing additional support you may not feel quite as large and awkward. After healing from birth many women find they feel more comfortable wearing a binder, corset or other compression garment to support their loose post-pregnancy skin and weak abdominal muscles.

What about underpants?

You may find underpants to be uncomfortable at times, so you may need to try a completely new style. As mentioned earlier, with your expanding abdomen you may want to try high-rise panties, "granny panties" or a bikini style. If you are not producing a discharge, you may even want to do without at times.

How big will I get?

"Am I a beached whale or an expectant mother of multiples on bedrest?"

Actually you can get quite large: larger than you can imagine. You may find that "normal" maternity clothes will not fit at some point. By the end you may not want to get dressed anyway. Some women who are petite fit into some plus size clothing, and some women wear a mumu type dress. If hospitalized, you can wear 1 or 2 gowns: one to cover the front and one the back. Your feet too can get quite large. You may find that you can only wear sandals in a larger size. Be careful wearing flip-flops or other shoes without a back. They can cause you to lose your balance and fall. After delivery your feet may actually stay a larger size but usually not as large as during pregnancy, so avoid buying many new shoes during pregnancy.

During this pregnancy your body is going through some dramatic changes. Embrace them even if you do not have the faintest recollection of who that person in the mirror is. What a rare and special gift this pregnancy is and your life thereafter truly will be.

How can I get comfortable?

As your pregnancy progresses you may find getting comfortable difficult to do. Try using several pillows while lying in bed to provide support. Place a pillow between your ankles, another between your knees, one behind your back, one under your belly, one or more under your head and then one under your arm. You can also use a body pillow, a longer than normal pillow, to help position yourself. Do not lie on your back as the weight of your uterus will compress the blood vessels in your abdomen and may, among other things, cause you to become light headed or feel dizzy. Of course, do not even attempt to lie on your stomach! As frequently as possible lie on your left side as this helps the blood flow to the uterus but do not lie on your left side only since you could develop skin breakdown (bed sores). An egg crate mattress, available with or without a prescription, may also help. Waterbeds are usually too hard to get out of, but in the early weeks of pregnancy you might find them comfortable.

How am I going to bathe or shave my legs?

Most women find getting out of a shower easier than getting into and out of a bathtub. Move slowly and carefully when showering as your balance is sometimes affected by the babies' weight and position. A chair or shower stool may be safer and make showering easier for you. We generally recommend using this at about 18 weeks, so you are not standing too long. You will know you are standing too much if you feel a pelvic pulling or drawing feeling. If your body feels like you need to sit down, sit down! Place a barstool between your bed and the bathroom so you can walk a little, and then sit before continuing to your goal.

You may need to use a shampoo/conditioner combination product when you shower to save time and steps. Feeling a bit light headed when coming out of a warm shower into the cool air of the bathroom is also not uncommon starting around 18-20 weeks for an expectant mother. You may want to consider showering when someone else is home and with the bathroom door open for better circulation of air. This way, if by chance you are lightheaded, someone else is there to help you if needed. After a while, and for those who are on complete bedrest, you may need to sponge bathe. Usually not the first choice, but it will work and you will feel "refreshed".

If you like to shave your legs, you will probably find that you cannot bend over your expanding belly to shave. You can ask someone else to shave them for you or just not worry about it. No one will care and you will not be able to see them anyway. The same is true for haircuts, hair coloring and makeup. Yes, it may make you feel better, but most everyone understands that you are doing something important like growing babies and may not be able to do these little things. Some expectant mothers feel better if they put on a little make-up or have a friend come to their home or hospital room and cut their hair or give a manicure. Just be sure you do not cut your cuticles because that opens your skin to infection.

What equipment can I buy to make life easier?

Some women borrow or buy a *reacher*. This is a long handled pole with a closing mechanism at one end operated by a trigger at the handle and is used to reach for and grab lightweight items. Whether or not you are on bedrest, this tool is helpful for picking up items dropped to the floor, arranging bedcovers or for grabbing something up high. You can purchase a reacher at pharmacies, medical supply stores, discount stores like Wal-Mart and Target or order online. Also helpful, especially for long legged women, is a raised toilet seat. Different styles are available and are designed to increase the toilet seat height to make it easier to sit down and stand up. Both of these items are sometimes covered by insurance if you doctor writes an order for them.

Preparing Your Family

Spouses and relatives often play an important role because you will likely need help with some, or many, of your activities before the babies are born and after. Some of your babies may need to stay in the hospital longer than others and you may need help caring for them at home after discharge. As much as you would like to be able to do everything, you cannot be everywhere all the time.

How Fathers and Significant Others Can Prepare

Unlike singleton births where the father may be less hands-on caring for his newborn, fathers of multiples need to become more involved immediately after delivery. Many fathers of multiples find themselves making decisions on behalf of the babies in the NICU while the mother recovers from a difficult pregnancy and Cesarean delivery. Fathers also serve a vital role in relaying updates to his wife before she can visit the babies. For most multiple birth families, the father continues to play a hands-on role caring for the babies after discharge. To care for so many high-need babies, mothers and fathers of multiples often form a very strong partnership in parenting. You and your spouse/significant other will need to decide an arrangement that works for you both. However, with more than one baby to care for, working together helps the mother recover and the babies to thrive.

Helping Older Siblings Prepare

"We have always tried to include our daughter as much as possible but did not push her if she did not want to participate. She has been amazing through the whole process and absolutely loves her siblings. We were VERY lucky we had no issues with her accepting the babies and how their arrival turned her life around."

There are many ways to help older siblings prepare for the arrival of multiples such as letting them help choose baby names or help with nursery preparations. If you chose to color-code items for your babies, older siblings can help chose those colors keeping one favorite color for themselves. For toddlers or preschoolers you may want to have the sibling dress in each of the babies' assigned colors, such as a colored shirt, or have them hold an item of that color and take pictures printing 2 copies of each. After delivery you can tape the appropriate picture to the new babies' hospital isolette so the sibling knows which ones are "his babies" as well as which baby is which when visiting. If you attach each photo to an index card and write a little something about the big sister or brother on it and then attach to the baby's isolette, the nurses will know a little bit more about your family and might even talk about older siblings to your babies in your absence. This will also help the nurses recognize the older siblings when they come to visit. Put the 2nd copy of the color photos on the refrigerator and then move them to the appropriate crib when each baby comes home so your older child(ren) knows exactly how many babies are left in the hospital and which ones are home.

If childcare is needed for siblings during the pregnancy, start by enlisting the help of friends and family. Determine a primary caregiver who can assume parental supervision in case you are hospitalized during pregnancy and most certainly at delivery. Having one person assume responsibilities can prevent mix-ups in childcare. Be sure this person is reliable, able and willing to assume these duties.

Also, arrange to have a backup available just in case complications arise. You should leave the pediatrician's number, the name of the local hospital preferred in case of an emergency, a copy of the child's insurance card and a medical release form authorizing this person to temporarily make medical decisions for a limited time if you cannot be reached. [See the Resources section at the end of this chapter for a link to a free medical release form on the MOST website.]

You can also evaluate daycare facilities and their ability to make special arrangements for extenuating circumstances such as during an unexpected hospitalization. For example, can the center make exceptions due to the situation such as move the child to the top of a waiting list or offer part-time care if they only offer full-time care? Can they make special financial arrangements? Some churches have daycare centers that are reasonably priced or offer scholarships.

You could contact local places of worship even if you are not a member. Many have volunteers who are able to assist with transportation, meals, childcare or other donations. Some volunteers might even continue to provide assistance when the new babies arrive if asked. In addition to places of worship, you can also contact your county health department to see if services are available through state-funded resources. Be sure to contact these agencies early to determine if siblings meet the eligibility criteria and to allow extra time to contact references about their level of satisfaction with individual programs. Some larger counties have volunteers to assist families. Your hospital social worker may help you identify other resources.

Regardless of who provides childcare coverage, the best predictors of childhood adjustment during such stressful periods is everyone's ability to maintain communication with the child and establish a routine. Make sure that consistent contact is made with the mother during hospitalizations. [See Chapter 6 for bedrest suggestions if you have an older child.]

Including Grandparents and Other Family Members

Grandparents and other family members are often willing and able to help you. To prepare them for the babies we suggest they read this book and visit the MOST website. Raising multiples and caring for preemies is different than it is for a singleton in many ways, so you may want to keep this in mind should you and your family members have different philosophies on child rearing and newborn/infant care. Right now you may not know how you are going to handle two, three or more babies, but you will learn. If your family members are willing to work with you, they can be very helpful. Sometimes family members move into the parent's home to assist with feedings, older siblings, diaper changing, laundry and even night feedings. They also may be willing to help watch older siblings and do routine household tasks while you are on bedrest. Sometimes this arrangement just will not work. Perhaps the grandparents or other family members are still employed or live far away. Perhaps you do not feel you want them to help, and that is okay too. Every family situation is different. Friends, neighbors and church members may be able and willing to help you instead.

Preparing Your Home

The amount of items needed for 2, 3, 4 or more babies may be hard to imagine. You may wonder how you are going to afford everything. Keep in mind that not all items have to be new, and you may not need one item for every baby. Some items can be previously used either by your older children or by other families. Larger items like cribs, activity centers and swings should be safety checked prior to use to ensure they have not been recalled. Buying new car seats is highly recommended because if the car seat has been in even a minor accident there may be damage that cannot be seen. Several shopping lists of items you may want to consider purchasing along with how many are usually needed are included later in this chapter.

Baby Showers

"I was really of two minds about this. I did not want to jinx our uneventful pregnancy by bringing all the baby stuff into the house, but I am also a planner and could not imagine not having everything ready when the babies came home. My control-challenged half took over, and I had a baby shower at about 23 weeks. After the babies came home I had another baby shower at my church in the town where I grew up and currently live. We were not able to attend this event, but we did receive many wonderful gifts."

Baby showers can be a special gift for expectant families of higher-order multiples. Even families with one or two older children may need additional items when expecting twins, triplets, quadruplets or more even if it is just diapers, baby bath or bibs. With the possibility of bedrest or an early delivery, timing a baby shower can be tricky. Some families, because of the high-risk nature of the pregnancy, are nervous about baby showers prior to 20 weeks gestation. Also expectant mothers of higher-order multiples are sometimes prescribed limited or complete bedrest starting around 22-25 weeks gestation and others are even hospitalized for the latter part of their pregnancy and therefore would be unable to attend. Friends or family members willing to host the event may not be aware of these scheduling hurdles or sure how to plan the event even if they do.

A poll on the MOST Family Support Forums showed that the vast majority, almost 90%, of families expecting triplets or more who had a shower did so, between 20 and 29 weeks gestation during the pregnancy, or they had one after delivery. Of course, each family situation is different and should be factored into planning a date, but this approach seemed to work best for most. For working mothers having a shower at the time they take maternity leave seems to work well. Several families reported attending their baby shower energized them to focus on their goal of delivering healthy babies.

"I had my shower at 24 weeks. I was on bedrest and had to get permission from my doctor with the assurance that I would rest until time to leave. I sat the entire time and let my friends wait on me hand and foot. Then I immediately went back to bed when I got home. It was really nice to get out of the house and be surrounded by friends and family."

Even with the best planning sometimes the event does not go as hoped, and many families expecting higher-order multiples have found ways to adapt. For some having a shower at their home worked well with volunteers to handle preparation and clean up. This approach allows the expectant mother to remain reclined on a couch or in a comfortable chair as well as have her own bed near-by while others help open gifts. This also eliminates traveling to and from the event. For others, having the event in their own home would be too stressful. Mothers who find themselves hospitalized prior to the shower may send the father-to-be or another family member or friend to be the guest of honor in their place. Pictures, video and special mementos like a guest-autographed photo of a sonogram later became cherished keepsakes from the event. A few mothers were even able to have a small shower in their hospital room.

Photo by Tom Hess

"My shower was planned for week 27, but I went into the hospital four days before and never came home until after the boys were born. My husband and older son were the stand-ins for me. I watched the video that someone took, and my husband did a great job oooohh-ing and ahhhh-ing over all the gifts....even the ones he was not sure what they would be used for!"

Whether by circumstance or choice, having a shower after delivery presents some unique challenges for families. Many still have babies in the NICU, and a few who experience a loss sometimes struggle to enjoy the occasion. Others worry about bringing the babies to the event because of the risk infection such as RSV or the logistical challenges of taking 3 or more tiny babies out of the house. To avoid that, some families work with the shower hostess to request guests who are sick or have been recently exposed to an illness not attend. Others, however, found a post-delivery shower to be the perfect option since they had stocked up on just the essentials (diapers, blankets, beds and basic clothing) beforehand and could now share their beautiful miracles with the many people who supported them through their pregnancy.

"We had our shower after the babies were born when they were about 5 months old and a little beyond RSV season. We wanted everyone to be able to see them, so the shower was at our church with the babies and all our family, etc. It was wonderful. I was too scared to have it before they were born, just too nervous that they might not all make it and then what would I do with all those adorable things."

Of course, not all families expecting higher-order multiples are given a baby shower. A poll in the MOST Family Support Forum Poll showed that 17% of families do not even have a baby shower. Families who have older children may prefer not to have a shower. Sometime circumstances, like being out of state for care or not having family members nearby, just do not make a shower possible. For those families many still received wonderful gifts after delivery.

"I did not have a shower. I went out of state for care at 20 weeks, so I was not around to attend. People gave us gifts, and at my husband's work they pooled for two double strollers, but we did not have a party. This was not my first baby, so I did have many things. But yes, I needed a few more!"

Here are a few ideas for unique baby showers that might be helpful to families expecting multiples.

- **Meal shower:** Guests bring frozen dinners in disposable containers with re-heating instructions or gift certificates with menus for restaurants that offer carryout or delivery options. If the shower is held too early to bring the actual dinners, guests can sign up on a fill-in calendar what meal they would like to bring and on what date. Ask a volunteer to call or email a reminder for meal date.

- **Disposable diaper, wipe and coupon shower:** Parents of multiples go through many disposable diapers and probably never have too many of these.

- **Baby safety shower:** A learning party where all the activities revolve around home safety themes. Developed by the Consumer Product Safety Commission. www.cpsc.gov/cpscpub/pubs/shower/shower.html.

Sometimes groups (from work, church or community) want to pool their contributions for one larger gift rather than several smaller gifts. Many times they will ask you or a family member what is needed. Strollers, car seats, a large chest freezer or washer and/or dryer are some items that families have needed that a group may be able to purchase.

Early preparation for the birth of multiples is a good idea, but parents may want to consider delaying major purchases until after delivery. Higher-order multiple pregnancies are risky up to the day of delivery. Sometimes the babies are born very early and, sadly, some families do not have an ideal outcome. In those situations purchases like major renovations, a new house or a new car can become long-term and heart-breaking reminders of what might have been.

Layette and Useful Equipment and Supplies

Clothing

You may not need all these items depending on your climate, the temperature of your living spaces, the time of year your babies are born and if you have a washer/dryer available. Although nice, all new clothing is not essential.

- 3 undershirts per baby.
- 2 Onesies per baby.
- 2 sleepers per baby.
- 2-3 gowns per baby.
- 2 caps/hats per baby: hospital may provide 1 or 2 each.
- 3-5 pairs of socks/booties per baby, more for cool weather. Infants do not need shoes.
- 1 snowsuit per baby if living in a very cold region.
- 20-30 small clothes hangers.
- 2 sweaters per baby.
- 1 sun hat per baby.
- 2 boxes/jugs of baby or additive free laundry soap.
- 1 small mesh laundry bag for small socks and clothing items.

Baby Equipment

- Multi-seat stroller(s). Some families buy triplet, quadruplet or quintuplet strollers and also use a double or single stroller to take babies one or two at a time or in conjunction with a baby sling or front-pack/back pack carriers. [See Resources section for link.]

- 1 or more activity gyms.

- Net cover for stroller to keep leaves and strangers hands from touching the babies.

- 1 or 2 baby swings. Swings can take up a lot of room when set up and are difficult to store and not all children like swings so try to borrow extras if you need them.

- 1 or 2 bouncy seats: you can borrow or buy extras if they prove helpful.

- 1 or 2 playpens or travel cribs

- Large play area gates and safety gates enough to block off safe area desired for infants/toddlers.

- 1 rear-facing infant car seat per baby.

Car seats must be used even when coming home from the hospital. Seats MUST be properly installed. **IT IS THE LAW!** Remember car seats are not recommended for any other purpose other than transporting in a vehicle. Babies sleeping in a car seat can stop breathing, so do not use infant/child car seats for sleeping without talking with your babies' health care provider. Infant car seats that have a carry handle usually fit preemies better than a larger convertible car seat. Some seats can attach to a stroller, available for two or three babies. Using an infant car seat with a carry handle also allows you to move the infants in and out of your car without waking unlike removing them from a backward facing convertible seat. Car seat manufacturers change styles often, so visit a few stores to see what styles are available. [See the Resources section at the end of this chapter for helpful websites links.]

Furniture

While deciding what furniture you may need you need to consider what will work best in your home. One nursery where all baby activity occurs (sleeping, diaper changing, dressing, etc) may not work for you. Some families find that a sleeping room (night time and nap time) that is upstairs will work if a main level room is used for changing diapers during the day, feeding and eventually play time. Families have used their dining room as the changing room, setting up additional cribs or pack-n-plays in there for daytime naps. Others have put the babies into the master bedroom and moved themselves to another bedroom. You may start with one plan and change it as the babies grow and your needs change.

- A rocking chair, glider or oversized recliner is useful particularly for nursing mothers. You may want to try these chairs before purchasing to make sure the height of the arm is high enough for you and comfortable to lean your arm on while feeding the babies.

- 1 crib for each baby. Be sure all mattresses are of a good quality and meet current safety requirements.

- 1 waterproof crib mattress cover and 2 quilted mattress pads per baby. *

- 4 crib sheets per baby (may want to try flannel sheets in the winter)*

- 4-5 receiving blankets per baby: waffle-weave blankets stretch nicely for swaddling.*

- 2 heavy blankets per baby and 1 large quilt/blanket for floor/tummy time.*

- Changing tables are helpful but not always essential. If you use them and you have a two-story home, you may want one for each floor of the house. A low dresser and padded top will also work fine, and some families even use entertainment systems where they install a tabletop that has a safety buckle. Be sure the height of the changing surface is suitable for you and does not cause additional strain on your back.

- 1 or 2 bassinets, cradles or Moses baskets can be borrowed and may be useful early on in two-story houses to have available for daytime naps.

- 1 large dresser or chest of drawers per child's room. Be sure to anchor to wall before babies are out of their cribs.

* Note: Bedding items needed may depend on your climate and washer/dryer availability

Diapering Supplies

- Start with 4-6 packages of newborn size disposable diapers. Some parents like to purchase preemie diapers; however many babies outgrow them before discharge or hospitals may even provide a few packages for parents to take home.

- Large diaper pails or trash cans that close securely: one for each changing station. Diaper pail rinse for cloth diapers. (Use 1/2 cup white vinegar per half pail full of water as a presoak; works as urine neutralizer for cloth diapers in a diaper pail.) Plastic trash bags or refills. Some families find a small trash can with plastic trash bags works the best. You will have lots of dirty diapers!

- 1 extra-large and 1 regular sized, for short trips, fully stocked diaper bags or backpacks. Some parents also keep a stocked bag in the car.

- 3 tubes of diaper rash cream/ointment.

- 3-4 waterproof lap pads per baby Parents who have babies in the NICU may want to request a few waterproof pads, also known as "chucks," to take home and use after discharge.

Bath Supplies

- 2 towels or hooded towels per baby.

- 3 washcloths per baby.

- 2 bottles baby lotion.

- 1 baby bath tub or large bath sponge for sink baths Note: bath rings are not recommended for safety reasons.

- 1 infant hair brush.

- Optional: 1 bottle mild baby soap for use on cradle cap. (Purchase a small size initially in case babies have allergies) Plain water baths are best for infants.

Feeding Supplies for Breastfeeding or Pumping

- Hospital-grade breast pump if pumping (can be rented). The hospital lactation consultant can help you locate one.

- Double nursing pillow if nursing. [See resources for link.]

- Milk storage bags or containers if pumping. The 2 oz containers provided by the NICU are nice, so parents may want to request some as well as the preemie nipples for use after discharge.

- 2 bottle and nipple brushes if pumping and storing milk.

- Manual/hand pump for quick trips.

- 4-5 nursing bras Note: you may want to wait until after delivery to determine the best fitting size.

- 7 nursing shirts if desired.

- 1 box of disposable or 4-5 sets of washable nursing pads.

- 8 - 8oz bottles for pumping breast milk once supply is established.

- 3 - 4oz bottles, nipples and rings per baby to feed babies when mother is not available.

- 6 bibs per baby: snap or Velcro bibs work best for young infants.

- 1 dozen cloth diapers per baby: useful as burp cloths.

- Quick, easy, healthy snacks, like breakfast bars for mother to eat while feeding or pumping.

- 2 sippy cups and spoons per baby.

- Several portable, spill proof water bottles for mother refilled frequently and placed at each of her nursing stations.

Feeding Supplies for Bottle Feeding

- 3 - 4oz bottles, nipples and rings per baby The 2 oz. containers provided by the NICU are nice, so parents may want to request some as well as the preemie nipples for use after discharge.

- 8 - 8oz bottles, nipples and rings per baby. Color coded for each baby if needed or use different color rubber bands or hair band holders.

- 4-cup measuring cup, whisk and 2 1-gallon liquid containers for measuring and mixing formula.

- 2 bottle and nipple brushes and 2 bottle trees for drying bottles.

- 1-2 dishwasher baskets to hold nipples and rings.

- 6 bibs per baby: snap or Velcro bibs work best for young infants.

- 1 dozen cloth diapers per baby: useful as burp cloths.

- 1 crock pot for warming bottles.

- 2 sippy cups per baby for use when babies are older.

- You may want to wait to buy formula until close to discharge since your health care provider may recommend a specific type. Shop around for the best prices or ask your nurse or primary health care provider to contact a formula representative on your behalf.

Medical Equipment

- Rectal thermometer and/or digital thermometer for axillary (under the arm) temperature taking. Check with the babies' doctor as he/she may recommend a certain method of temperature taking.

- Cotton swabs and balls.

- Rubbing alcohol for belly button care if recommended by your health care provider.

- Petroleum jelly.

- Fully stocked first aid kit including phone number to poison control.

- 1 nasal aspirators-bulb for removing mucus from the nose. You may get them free from the hospital. Label each of them with a baby name or initials so you use only one per child.

- Baby nail scissors.

- 3 bottles infant fever reducers like Acetaminophen as recommended by your baby's health care provider.

- 1 medicine syringe per baby labeled with baby's name or initials.

- Humidifier or vaporizer if recommended by your babies' primary health care provider.

Other Supplies

- Log book to track feedings, diaper changes, medications, etc. [See Resources section at the end of this chapter for link.]

- Age-appropriate toys like a mobile (until baby can pull up), board books, rattles, teethers, stuffed animals, etc. Buy a variety of textures, sounds, colors, etc. No toys should be left in the crib while baby is sleeping there.

- Nightlight(s) or soft light or dimmer lamp

- Baby monitor/camera/intercom (if desired) Consider buying a monitor that has two receivers so you can place them in different areas of the house: like your bedroom and the kitchen.

- 1 baby book per child to record day-to-day milestones. Some parents use a large space calendar to record milestones to enter into the baby book later. If you have an older child, you may want to get the exact same baby book if available so that you can update his/hers at the same time and in the same format.

- Camera/video camera and batteries/charger for them

- Smoke detectors, carbon monoxide detectors placed in every bedroom and on every floor. Call your local fire department for recommendations.

- Bottle of hand soap or hand sanitizer and conditioning hand lotion at every sink. Keep hand sanitizers out of reach of children as they can result in alcohol poisoning.

- Fire extinguisher on every floor

- A small refrigerator for the nursery for pumping mothers or for two-story homes to store night-time bottles. This is optional but nice to have.

- Cordless or cell phone

- Answering machine/voicemail

- Birth announcements: prepare address list before delivery

- Lullaby music

- Battery recharger/rechargeable batteries for equipment and toys

In addition to the list of supplies listed above we are including a list of items below that we recommend parents do not purchase. Some items pose a danger or risk to your babies, and others are just not useful enough to be worth their high cost. Of course, each family's needs are unique, but we encourage you to learn more about the safety of any item used for your babies before purchasing it.

Items NOT to Buy

- Padded head rests for car seats that are not part of the original car seat. Even items like this that are part of the seat may need to be removed for proper positioning especially for preemies. Instead use two tightly rolled towels, cloth diapers or baby blankets; one on each side of the head and trunk. Additional towels, diapers, etc. can be used if needed for snug support. Check with the nurses prior to discharge for their recommendation.

- Sun shields for car windows - may pose a projectile hazard in the event of an accident.

- Jumper devices - these are not recommended for preemies.

- Digital ear thermometers - these devices are not as accurate as needed and can be expensive.

- Baby powder - small particles can be hazardous to an infant's lungs.

- Non-stationary walkers - pose a variety of safety hazards for babies including serious falls and should not be used.

- Bumper pads, crib comforters or any soft bedding - these items are not recommended due to the risk of Sudden Infant Death Syndrome (SIDS).

- Infant bath seats that attach to the side or bottom of the tubs - these pose a risk of drowning.

- Sleep positioners as these wedge-shaped pieces of foam meant to keep infants in a side sleeping position - may increase the risk of suffocation.

- Over-the-counter infant or children's cold or cough medication - products have not been proven effective in children under the age of 6 and have resulted in the deaths, even at proper dosage, in children.

- Crib dividers – which can increase the risk of suffocation.

- Twin/triplet baby carriers: front or backpack - carriers can be awkward to use and the babies often get heavy too quickly to use them enough.

- Car mirrors that allow the driver to see baby(ies) while driving - pose a driving hazard and should not be used.

Resources

Finding Help or Childcare

- The MOST booklet *Childcare for Multiples* contains resources, tips and information about helpers, in-home childcare and childcare centers: www.MOSTonline.org/sunshop/index.php?l=product_detail&p=75.

- Lotsa Helping Hands is a web site that allows you (or someone else) to manage volunteers, meals, babysitting, rides, errands, yard work or anything else your family needs while you are on bedrest, hospitalized or the babies are young. It is a free online program found at: www.lotsahelpinghands.com.

- MOST article for volunteers titled "Tips for Helping a New Family of Multiples": www.MOSTonline.org/sunshop/index.php?l=product_detail&p=327

Product Safety and Medical Release Forms

- See the Consumer Product Safety Commission's Electronic Reading room for more information on baby product safety: www.cpsc.gov/cgi-bin/foia.aspx

- Sign up for their free product recall alerts from the Consumer Product Safety Commission: www.cpsc.gov/cpsclist.aspx.

- See this site for more information about the safe use of infant jumpers: www.consumerreports.org/cro/baby-jumpers/buying-guide.htm

- MOST offers a FREE medical release form authorizing someone to temporarily make medical decisions if you cannot be reached at: www.MOSTonline.org/membersonly/emergency.htm

Breastfeeding

- Frequently Asked Questions: http://www.mostonline.org/faq_bf.htm
- MOST's Breastfeeding Multiples booklet offers in-depth information, tips, resources, and more on breastfeeding multiples. www.mostonline.org/sunshop/index.php?l=product_detail&p=80
- MOST's Infant Multiples Booklet also offers breastfeeding resources www.mostonline.org/sunshop/index.php?l=product_detail&p=74.
- FDA breast pump information: www.fda.gov, search for breast pumps

Feeding Charts, Color Coding and Getting Organized

- Free samples of feeding logs for multiples are available on the MOST website at: www.MOSTonline.org/membersonly/feedchart.htm
- Learn more about color-coding in the MOST Infant Multiples Packet: www.mostonline.org/sunshop/index.php?l=product_detail&p=74

Car Seats

- For general information on car seats, infant seats and boosters visit: www.cpsafety.org
- Seat Check website: www.seatcheck.org/ or call 1-866-SEAT-CHECK for information on car seat installation.
- Car Seat Data provides buying guides, guidelines on car seat/vehicle compatibility, car seat FAQs, where to find a certified car seat inspector and how to assess a car seat's installation. It has one of the most useful resources for parents of multiples: a data sheet listing the measurements for dozens of the most common car seats on the market to help parents determine whether 3, 4, 5 or more seats will fit: www.CarSeatData.org

- MOST Supertwins 101 FAQ on car seats and multiples: www.MOSTonline.org/faq42.htm

Chapter 8: Delivery

Finally the big day has come! Whether delivering today is by choice or necessity, the babies are coming! Here is some information about delivery. Talk with your doctor and nurses about what will happen at delivery. Ask them to describe to you and your husband how the delivery room is set up and what will occur. If possible request to have a Lamaze and C-section class in advance. If you are at home on bedrest ask for information on who locally is affiliated with your hospital and available to come to your home to provide this class. If you are hospitalized for an extended period prior to delivery ask if you can receive this class at bedside. Even though you will most likely be having a C-section knowing Lamaze breathing can be very helpful throughout labor and during recovery. If you have had a vaginal delivery with an older child a refresher class with C-section information can be very helpful and reassuring. Some questions to discuss before delivery include:

1. What is allowed in the delivery room: music, photography, videotaping? How many family members can be in the delivery room?

2. Do you want your infants' umbilical cord blood collected? Although not a standard procedure, some parents choose to collect and store some of their infants' umbilical cord blood. If you are interested in this option contact the Cord Blood Registry at 1-888-932-6568 or http://cordblood.com.

Vaginal Delivery of Higher-Order Multiples

According to the MOST Medical Birth survey 3.8% of mothers gave birth vaginally and another 1.8% had a combined vaginal/C-section birth. Risks associated with a vaginal birth in a multiple pregnancy include:

- Difficulty monitoring all babies during active labor
- Difficultly determining which baby is in distress
- An increased risk of stillbirth
- Excessive maternal bleeding
- Damage to the pelvic floor (uterus, bladder, rectum)

Vaginal delivery may be possible for some triplet pregnancies although the vast majority will require a Cesarean birth. Women who have had prior successful vaginal deliveries are better candidates for a vaginal delivery of triplets. Vaginal delivery of quadruplets or more is not recommended. The minimal criteria for considering a vaginal delivery of triplets are:

- Vertex (head down) presentation of the presenting triplet (baby closet to the cervix)
- Ability to continuously monitor all three triplets during labor
- Lack of any contraindications to vaginal delivery

These 3 criteria are based upon published studies which generally did not put limits on gestational age or fetal weight; however, your doctor may require your pregnancy to reach a certain gestation to consider a vaginal delivery. A vaginal delivery should only be attempted by practitioners experienced with the following:

- Vaginal delivery of triplets
- Ultrasound techniques to assess the babies' status in-utero during labor
- Turning a baby to a different position in-utero prior to delivery
- C-sections

All babies should be monitored continuously prior to delivery to track fetal heart rates. Adequate anesthesia should be used if babies B or C should require in-utero manipulation to a vertex position; an epidural anesthetic is ideal. An anesthesiologist should also attend at the delivery and prepared for an emergency Cesarean birth or the need to administer uterine relaxants. Finally, the delivery should be performed in a room equipped to perform a Cesarean delivery. [19] Discuss your doctor's experience and outcomes of prior vaginal triplet deliveries.

C-Sections & Combined Deliveries

According to the MOST Medical Birth survey 93.4% of mothers give birth to their triplets, quadruplets or more by C-section, and as noted above, only 3.8% of mothers gave birth vaginally and another 1.8% via a combined vaginal/C-section birth. For 1% of respondents type of delivery was not stated. A combined delivery involves the delivery of one or more babies vaginally followed by the delivery of one or more babies via C-section whether due to an unexpected vaginal preterm birth or to address complications that arise during a planned vaginal delivery. This may also happen during a delayed interval delivery. [See section later in this chapter for more information on delayed interval deliveries.]

Scheduled C-Section versus Emergency C-Section

Your doctor, most likely, will schedule a C-section when he/she feels it is the optimal time to deliver the babies. This date may change to an earlier or later date as your health and the babies' health changes. A scheduled C-section ensures that Labor & Delivery and the NICU are adequately staffed for the births of the babies. Sometimes it is not possible to have a scheduled C-section and an emergency C-section is necessary. Your doctor may diagnose distress in one of the babies or you may develop a condition that requires immediate delivery of the babies.

Staff Members Present during a C-Section for Multiples

Personnel may vary depending on the gestation at delivery and the facility:

- One anesthesiologist
- One delivery nurse
- One or more surgeons (OB/GYN or Perinatologist)
- Surgical nurse for each surgeon
- Neonatologist for each baby
- Neonatal Nurse for each baby
- Possibly a Respiratory Therapist for each baby

A C-section delivery will usually take no more than 5 minutes, but the stitching of your incision will take about 45 minutes or more. You may not be able to see the babies right after delivery if they require immediate medical attention, but you will usually be able to see them briefly before they are cleaned.

Anesthesia during Delivery

You will most likely be given an epidural prior to your delivery. After cleansing the lower spine you will be numbed with an anesthetic before the actual epidural needle is placed. The needle is removed and a thin plastic tube is left in place and taped down. The medications that provide the numbing effect are given through that tube as needed during delivery and recovery. Some women feel that the needle insertion is uncomfortable while others feel it is painful. Some will not feel it at all, but the medications will soon relieve any pain that you have. A spinal block (also referred to as a spinal or spinal anesthesia) is one shot injected directly into the spinal fluid. This also decreases your pain sensation but you may still feel some tugging or other mild sensations. Both epidurals and spinal blocks relieve the pain during a C-section. General anesthesia is usually only used in some emergency C-sections. With general anesthesia you will be unconscious and have no pain or other sensations. According to MOST statistics:

- 55.2% were given epidural anesthesia
- 34.4% were given spinal anesthesia
- 5.7% were given general anesthesia
- 4.7% were given no anesthesia, local anesthesia, or did not answer

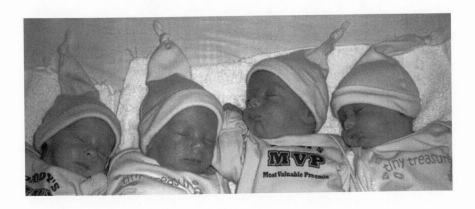

Delayed Interval Deliveries

Unbelievably different delivery dates are possible with multiples. One MOST family actually has a set of triplets who were born in different centuries! Two babies were born on Dec. 31, 1999 and the third was born on Jan. 1, 2000. Aside from babies born around midnight, which results in different birthdays, some mothers have what is known as a delayed interval delivery (DID). A delayed interval delivery is when a mother pregnant with multiples goes into preterm labor and gives birth to one or more babies but a few days or weeks later gives birth to the remaining babies. After the birth of the first baby, labor stops progressing on its own or through the use of medical intervention. The pregnancy is then continued in hopes that the remaining baby(ies) can be born at a later gestation with fewer complications.

A DID may be an option when one or more babies is born prior to viability or extremely prematurely (24 weeks or earlier) and the goal is for the remaining babies to reach an age when their chances of survival increase. A DID may also be an option if the first baby is born at a later gestational age (25 weeks gestation or later) when it might allow the mother to deliver at an even later gestation so the remaining baby(ies) have fewer complications due to prematurity. Your doctor should discuss with you the benefits and risks in attempting a DID. Among the factors that influence whether a DID would be attempted are the presentation of each baby (head-down versus breech) and the mother's risk of infection.

If a DID is attempted, hospitalization, medications to prevent contractions, placement of a cerclage and other interventions may be used. Parents facing the option of a DID should understand that the outcome will depend on a number of factors including the reason for delivery of the first baby, the gestation of the pregnancy, chances of infection, and interventions used. Whether any of the babies will benefit from a DID is uncertain. Although the odds are slim, MOST has worked with a number families who have had success with a DID. Their remaining babies were delivered at later gestations with fewer complications than if all babies had been delivered when the first infant was born.

Postpartum Recovery

"I had to get magnesium sulfate at delivery since I had developed preeclampsia. I was unable to get on my feet for 48 hours to see the babies. I vaguely remember visiting the NICU on a gurney and saying, 'Okay, there is one. Where is the next one and the next one?' I only stayed about 5 minutes total and did not hold any of them. I was too weak and worried I would drop them. I worried that I would not bond with them but really did not have any problem."

As with any other surgical procedure many mothers experience shaking in the recovery room, but warm blankets may help. You should expect to spend one or more hours in the recovery room and usually your support person can visit you after a short while. Rarely do mothers need a blood transfusion due to the amount of blood lost during delivery. Post-surgery you may have:

- Pain located at incision site or the back if you had spinal or epidural anesthesia. (It is okay to request pain medication!)

- Gas pain in the stomach, due to bloating, that radiates to the shoulder and neck. Walking and rolling on the bed helps relieve this gas pain. As soon as you are allowed to have fluids drink as much hot or room temperature water with lemon as possible to help pass the gas. Aim for 4 to 6 cups a day. Squeeze the juice from half a lemon into the cup of water.

- Bleeding due to shedding of the uterine lining material (locchia). The bleeding may last longer following the birth of multiples than a singleton.

- If you received magnesium sulfate at delivery because of preeclampsia, you most likely will have the side effects noted previously (hot flashes, dizziness, fogginess, etc.) This drug can make it hard for you to see your babies in the NICU.

Sometimes you will not be able to visit your babies right after delivery. If this is the case, perhaps your husband, friend or family member could take photos with a cell phone or digital camera and bring them to you. Even though it may be heart breaking to not see your babies, do not worry; you will bond with them soon. When you do meet your babies you may feel overwhelmed or like a bystander since the NICU staff is caring for them at this moment. Some women have said that they had a panic attack since all of those worries over the last few months had finally been relieved and the babies were finally here. You may cry. You may just smile. All of these responses are common and normal. You may feel better talking about your feelings with your husband, nurse, social worker, member of your clergy or doctor. Let them know how you are feeling.

Most mothers will start passing clots (sized from a gumball to a tangerine) about 7-10 days after delivery. In most cases this is normal, but let your doctor know if this happens. You may notice that your bleeding will start to slow down about this time (7-10 days post-delivery). However, it can continue much longer for some. If you are very active, you may notice your flow get heavier. This is a signal you are doing too much so slow down and rest.

Leaving the Hospital: You and Your Babies

You will probably be discharged before any of the babies. Many mothers find it hard to leave their babies at the hospital even if they knew ahead of time the babies would be staying in the NICU for a while. Trust that the nurses and doctors will take good care of them. Take some time to rest and recover. You did a great job! Your body will need time to recuperate from pregnancy, bedrest and surgery. The doctors and nurses may not be able to estimate how long the babies will be in the hospital because that depends on many factors: gestational age at birth, development, birth defects, infections, etc. If the doctors or nurses do give you a date, remember this is an estimate or educated guess. Your baby(ies) may remained hospitalized longer or leave sooner depending on how he or she grows, test results and other factors. Infants must be able to maintain body temperature, breathe on their own and in most cases feed from a bottle or breast. [See Chapter 1 for average length of hospital stays.]

Although weight gain is important, premature infants are not released from the NICU based on a set weight goal. Frequently one baby will be discharged at a time, so you may have one or more babies at the hospital and one or more babies at home. You may feel guilty because you do not spend enough time with any of them, but do not let these feelings take over! You cannot be in all places at all times. Your babies will all love you. Take this time to recover because once they are home you will be busy. Mothers should be aware that recovery from a higher-order multiple pregnancy might require weeks, or even, months.

While the NICU can be a stressful experience for many parents, there is a variety of resources available to you. If you have not already ordered a copy of the

MOST Infant Multiples booklet, this would be a good time to do that. The booklet is a comprehensive resource for parents of infant multiples filled with pertinent information about the NICU, discharge, and managing babies at home. The packet contains information on infant feeding, a grams-pounds weight conversion chart, frequently asked questions, feeding/diaper/medication charts, developmental milestones, Early Intervention, postpartum depression, choosing a pediatrician, and much, much more. You might also want to review the section "What to Look for in a Level III NICU" in Chapter 2 of this book to find a checklist on discharge preparation for parents and other caregivers. Another great resource is PreemieCare. PreemieCare is a non-profit division of MOST dedicated to supporting families of infants born preterm through education, support, and resources. You can also share your experiences and find support by visiting the MOST Family Support Forums on the MOST website. Feel free to contact the MOST office directly if you have questions or concerns. We are happy to help families through the NICU experience and beyond. [See Chapter 10 of this book for details on how to find all of these and additional resources.]

'Full-Term' or Late Preterm Babies

A baby born after 39 weeks gestation is considered term and referred to as a term baby. A baby born between 37 and 39 weeks gestation is considered *early term*. Births before 37 weeks are premature. **Many twin babies and the vast majority of higher-order multiple birth babies, which are triplets or more, are born premature**. It is important for you to remember that no matter what gestational week your babies are born, if they are born before 37 weeks, they are premature. Every premature baby is at risk for developmental challenges, medical challenges and educational challenges during their childhood. Risks for a late preterm baby born at 34 weeks are much less than for one born at 28 weeks, but there are areas of development that need to be watched over the years. Preemies are still are at risk for RSV (respiratory syncytial virus), SIDS and subtle learning challenges later in life. [Refer to chart in chapter 2 titled "Average Days Infants Were Hospitalized after Birth by Gestation and Type."]

If you are fortunate enough to carry your babies until 35+ weeks gestation, congratulations! Your babies may not spend much time in the hospital, but what does that mean for you? You may need just as much help at home as someone with very premature babies as you may not have much time to recover physically from the pregnancy and C-section. Even though you delivered healthy, albeit tiny newborns, infection prevention (hand washing and not allowing caretakers/visitors who are sick in the home) is still very important as your babies are at risk for RSV. You may not have much time to learn CPR and what follow up care is needed. Even though these babies will seem like smaller full-term infants, they are still premature. They do not need to "just grow a little" to be like a full-term infant.

No matter what gestational age your babies are born and no matter how uneventful the delivery and NICU course is, you still need to remember that your babies have some risk and you will need to be proactive in avoiding illnesses and having each developmentally assessed regularly for the first 3 years.

References

(19) D C Jones, "Triplet Pregnancy: Mid and Late Pregnancy Complications and
      Management," in UpToDate,
          http://www.uptodate.com/patients/content/topic.do?topicKey=~2H5HS
          mX6VO_BmG (accessed December 14, 2006).

Chapter 9: Practical Considerations

During the pregnancy and after the babies are born, you and your partner may feel stressed. This pregnancy and the care of these babies is life changing. This chapter will discuss personal and marital stress, insurance and financial concerns and postpartum depression in the mother. We strongly urge you to talk with counselors, clergy, social workers or mental health workers to help you build a strong family.

Personal and Marital Stress

"I have been in tears the past few days as I feel like such a helpless person relying on everyone to do it all for me. It is making me crazy! I cannot even put on my socks or shoes anymore. I told my husband that soon he would have to put my underwear on for me since I cannot bend easily to get them on! It is quite frustrating."

Having a baby is an emotional roller coaster for all parents. Parents of twins, triplets, quadruplets, quintuplets or more may experience many of the same emotions as parents of singletons, but their roller coaster is more intense and often conflicted. The joys of one baby doing well may be overshadowed by the setbacks of another baby or the complications of yet another. The range of emotions felt at one time can be overwhelming. Having babies who are still hospitalized after you are discharged may seem unnatural especially after such a long and trying pregnancy. Stress may make bonding with babies difficult for both parents. During the pregnancy, NICU stay and beyond and you may experience feelings such as:

1. **Loss of Independence** – particularly during bedrest but also in the months following birth when outings can be difficult or risky to preterm infants. Parents should remember that this loss of independence is only temporary. The babies are not babies forever! Whenever someone offers you time-away use the opportunity to refresh yourselves and your marriage.

2. **Inadequacy** – many parents of multiples feel they are not up to the challenge of caring for so many fragile babies, but almost all of these

parents find their own unique way of coping, surviving and even thriving in their new role.

3. **Isolation or Being Different** – a feeling that begins during pregnancy and may linger for many years. Connecting with other families of higher-order multiples or parents of preemies can be very helpful.

4. **Being Misunderstood** – also common during bedrest when others may view this as a life of luxury or note the attention and outpouring of help and gifts for families of multiples. Just remember that bedrest is often a critical part of a high-risk and/or higher-order multiple pregnancy and eventually the other attention fades. Parents must remain focused on the important task at hand: growing healthy babies.

5. **Major Shift in Household Responsibilities** – this may apply especially to partners while the mother is on bedrest, hospitalized, or for some time after delivery but again is temporary. Consider getting outside help if needed.

6. **Frustration or Loss** – feeling frustrated or that you have lost the chance to have a "normal" pregnancy, birth or parenting experience. The guarded optimism during the pregnancy and early weeks or months while the babies are in the NICU can be frustrating or may feel like yet another form of loss even when family and friends offer support and encouragement that "everything will be okay." Though most multiple birth pregnancies end well, this is not always the case. When feelings of frustration or loss start to overwhelm parents, they should try to focus on the positives, seek support from family and friends and maybe consider counseling during this time. Talking with other MOST families on the MOST website forums can be very helpful.

7. **Financial Struggle** – families of multiples often face the loss of one parent's income, substantial medical bills and/or paying a significant cost for childcare. That coupled with all the additional costs for equipment, food, diapers and other expenses often intensify stress for

multiple birth parents. Parents should accept offers to help financially or with other tasks both during pregnancy and while the babies are small. This phase too will pass. While saving for college and retirement may always be a big challenge for parents of multiples, many families develop some amazing dollar-stretching skills that allow them to catch up once they pass the demanding infant phase.

Coping with the Stress of Parenting Multiples

While a high-risk pregnancy or caring for so many babies can be stressful on a relationship, parents of higher-order multiples or preemie twins often form a very strong partnership in parenting which can strengthen their bond. Some stress and disagreement between couples may not even be related to the birth of their multiples. Do not hesitate to contact someone to help both of you. [See the Resources section at the end of this chapter to learn more about the MOST 'Divorce and the Multiple Birth Family' survey.] Parents might find the following tips helpful when coping with the stresses of a high-risk pregnancy or parenting multiples:

- Explore how you have handled other crises and what helped.
- Spend some time picking names for the babies to help build a connection.
- Recognize that feeling stunned, frightened and overwhelmed is normal.
- Focus on positive progress during the pregnancy and NICU stay; mothers in particular tend to feel guilty that they could not carry the babies longer.
- Remember to take care of yourself and each other physically by getting enough food and rest to keep up health and spirits.
- Build each other's mental well-being through good communication and acknowledging that each partner may have separate needs and may handle the situation differently.
- Express your emotions in a safe place by crying, screaming, getting angry, being afraid, etc.
- Do not forget that walking or other physical activities (if allowed for the mother) can help work off fear and other emotions. Sometimes one or both

parents need to remove themselves from the tension temporarily to regroup.

- Writing letters to yourself, other children or the babies is a good way to work through emotions.
- Talk to family members, friends, support groups, religious leaders, social workers and professional counselors if needed.
- Always believe in miracles!

Insurance and Financial Concerns

"Everything looked great until my husband told his colleague at work I was pregnant with triplets. His colleague of course had the same insurance and shared that their last child was a preemie, and they discovered that, while the NICU was covered, the DOCTORS in the NICU were not. They ended up with an $89,000 bill! I immediately opted for COBRA with the insurance from my job. It was expensive but I did not want any more surprises. Be sure to check your insurance policy so you understand what aspects of your and your babies' care will be covered."

As new parents or soon to be parents the first step is to consider where you want to be as a family in 5 years. To be happy and healthy most families need to plan. Freeing up any finances available to make life easier is very important in the short term especially during the first year. You will have extra expenses like medical bills, baby equipment, diapers etc., so look for expenses you can cut such as cable television, an expensive vehicle, etc. You may need to put less money into savings temporarily as well as take other measures. This can give you options for hired help, ready-made food and household services that can make life less stressful.

As the first year or two passes families can then start developing long-term financial goals to meet such needs as their children's education, childcare, and most importantly, their own retirement. One of the first obstacles for many families financially is dealing with medical bills and insurance issues. The road to getting all of this resolved has the potential to be long and frustrating and can often feel like a second job. You do have rights and there are people on your side. Below are some quick tips to getting through the confusion:

1. **Breathe In, Breathe Out. Repeat** - Take a deep breath and realize that you are not alone and that you will get through this. Some insurance claims can take up to a year to be completely resolved.

2. **Get Organized** - Invest in a simple school notebook to keep notes on everything as it progresses. On the inside front cover of the notebook write a list of the various providers, their phone numbers, addresses and office hours. You can use large envelopes or a set of folders to divide the insurance Explanation of Benefits (EOB) by provider and organize from there.

3. **Professionalism** - Consider your medical providers your friends. They want to make sure their practice is paid, so chances are that they have not only been through this before with other patients, but may have some sort of template appeals letter they can provide to you. All conversations with the provider should be polite and professional. That way you become less of an account number and more of a human

being. Every time you call the customer service department of the insurance company be prepared with questions and all documents necessary. If you have a speakerphone at home or work, use it to allow you to write notes easily and access information they may need.

4. **Take Notes** - Take notes on every phone call and make sure to include the date, time and the person you spoke with asking for full name and correct spelling.

5. **Persistence Pays Off** - You have the right to challenge a denied claim, so if a simple phone call to the insurance company does not work, you can write an appeal letter.

In addition to regular health insurance, purchasing supplemental insurance during your pregnancy is one way to cover additional costs. [See insurance resources at the end of this chapter.] Note however that these types of insurance policies are not available in all states or to all families for the NICU or multiple birth coverage. Some supplemental insurance policies are only offered through employer groups and some are offered to individuals, so be sure to check what options are available to you.

Postpartum Depression

Many woman experience mood changes following childbirth which sometimes include periods of feeling blue that resolve without treatment. For up to 25% of mothers of multiples, however, these symptoms can last longer and may require treatment. Specifically postpartum depression (PPD) is officially defined as a period of severe depression following childbirth most often occurring between 4 weeks and 2 years postpartum.

Many mothers of multiples deny symptoms of PPD or fail to seek treatment due to a feeling that they should be happy to have these babies after all the effort required to become pregnant or maintain their pregnancy. Many mothers report feeling that they "do not have the right to be depressed" or feel guilty about addressing their symptoms with the health care provider who worked so hard to help them become a mother. Experiencing these feelings is common and your health care provider will respond in a positive and supportive manner. Research by MOST and other researchers has shown that symptoms of PPD may be more common in mothers of multiples and could present with different symptoms compared to mothers of singletons. Specifically, mothers of multiples indicated feeling more anxious or overwhelmed, having a loss of interest in activities and feeling more irritable and agitated. [See resources at the end of this chapter.]

If you or your family have concerns about how you are feeling, a screening by a health care professional is an important first step that can help determine if you might benefit from treatment for depression. If you have concerns about how you are feeling, please be sure to discuss this with your provider. A list of additional resources is listed at the end of this chapter. If you should have any further questions, please contact your health care provider or the MOST office.

Do I Have PPD?

Symptoms include feeling sad, loss of interest in activities and/or children, withdrawal from others, fatigue, appetite changes, sleep disturbance, feelings of worthlessness, irritability, restlessness, difficulty making decisions and thoughts of suicide. Any of the symptoms may occur suddenly or have a gradual onset. Fluctuations in appetite changes and sleep impairments commonly occur among all new mothers. A health care practitioner can screen for PPD with a short interview and/or brief screening test to determine if your symptoms represent common fluctuations after pregnancy or PPD.

Why Should I Seek Treatment?

As a mother to many children you owe it to yourself and your family to seek treatment so you are at your best for your children, spouse and yourself. You have gone to great lengths and made many sacrifices to bring these children into the world and now need to be at your best to continue being the mother you wish to be. Research has shown that PPD typically does not resolve without treatment. Depression can have a devastating impact on mothers, children and families. Studies have shown that mothers suffering with PPD are less likely to bond with their infant(s) and interact less with their child(ren). In addition, children of mothers who suffered with PPD are more likely to have intellectual, social and psychiatric problems. Furthermore, marital problems are more likely in families suffering with PPD. In the most severe cases, untreated PPD can result in the mother fatally injuring herself and/or her child(ren).

Important Note: If you are having thoughts of harming yourself or your child, seek immediate assistance. Any hospital or health care provider can assist you in arranging the services that you may need.

What Treatments are Available?

Medications, individual and group therapy, peer support groups and combinations of treatment options are available. Check with your provider and insurance carrier for treatment options. Remember to select the one that best suits you.

Online Safety and Security for Your Family

The Internet is an excellent place to share your pregnancy news and your journey with friends and family, but you may want to consider the ramifications of divulging too much personal information. Several families of multiples have had photos of their children or their family story stolen by individuals who, for various reasons, wish to impersonate or pretend to be a family of multiples. In addition, for many years a man has solicited information from families of triplets or more through a variety of techniques, most recently online. His primary focus has been to obtain photos and details about the size of the mother's pregnant belly. He will pretend to be a "husband" of a woman pregnant with multiples (usually the number that you have), a "researcher" studying multiple birth or even a "mother" wanting to know what to expect.

Be cautious about sharing names, date of birth, grandparents names, photos, or other personal data with individuals who contact you by phone or online (blogs, Facebook, etc.). If you believe a suspicious individual has contacted you or used your information, please contact MOST and let us know the details of your experience so we can take measures to protect and warn other families of multiples. In addition, once your information and photos are accessible on the Internet, you should consider them publically available for the foreseeable future. Even though you delete facts and photos, the information may have been stored somewhere or cached by a search engine like Google or Yahoo, so it can resurface at any time. [If you are looking for more information about working with the media or online safety, see the resources at the end of this chapter.]

Online support groups can also have members that falsify their family status. They sometimes pretend to be pregnant to obtain goods or money. Various forums and websites can be helpful for support but be cautious about obtaining medical advice. Look for websites that are HONcode certified. These sites need to meet strict criteria regarding the information they publish.

Some families have also found that securing new employment was complicated by the publicity of their multiple pregnancy. Prospective employers often search the Internet for information about future employees. Since the care of premature infants can pose a financial burden and/or increased insurance needs, some companies may be deterred from hiring an individual pregnant with multiples or parents who are caring for preterm multiples. The key point is that you should be careful about what you share online and in other forms of media such as newspapers and TV. [See resources at the end of this chapter for more details on personal information and media.]

Resources

Marital Stress and Multiples

- See statistics and findings from the MOST 'Divorce and the Multiple Birth Family' survey: www.MOSTonline.org/facts_divorcesurvey.htm

- Join the MOST forums to post questions on our Marriage and Family forum: www.MOSTonline.org/forums.htm

Postpartum Depression

- Your health care provider and your children's pediatrician are sources for information

- MOST PPD study statistics: www.MOSTonline.org/facts_PPDSurvey.htm

- MOST Supertwins FAQ on PPD: www.MOSTonline.org/faq16.htm

- MOST *SUPERTWINS* article on PPD: www.MOSTonline.org/sunshop/index.php?l=product_detail&p=63

- MOST resource links on PPD: www.MOSTonline.org/links.htm#Postpartum_Depression

- National Suicide Prevention Lifeline is a 24-hour, confidential, toll-free suicide prevention service: 1-800-273-TALK (8255)

- Postpartum Support International: www.postpartum.net/ or 1-800-994-4PPD

Insurance and Medical Bills

- The Patient Access Network Foundation is a non-profit organization that helps families pay out-of-pocket costs associated with certain diagnoses. This currently includes costs for RSV prevention and treatment: www.panfoundation.org/ or 1-866-316-PANF (7263)

- To locate free or low cost health insurance coverage in your state contact Insure Kids Now. Run by the US Department of Health & Human Services. You can call confidentially 1-877-KIDS-NOW: www.insurekidsnow.gov/

- Learn more about the Family and Medical Leave Act (FMLA): www.dol.gov/dol/topic/benefits-leave/fmla.htm or 1-866-4-USWAGE

- Patient Advocate Foundation is a national non-profit organization focused on patient advocacy that helps patients through mediation to care: www.patientadvocate.org/ or 1-800-532-5274

- Patients are Powerful is a national non-profit organization focused on patient advocacy that provides items such as online printable sample letters to deal with health insurances issues: www.patientsarepowerful.org/ or (916) 652 2293

- Supplemental insurance policies (such as Aflac: www.aflac.com) can provide additional money for expenses when a mother is hospitalized prior to delivery or while infants are in the NICU.

- Additional financial and insurance related resources are available at: www.MOSTonline.org/preemieBB/viewforum.php?f=76

Personal Information and the Media

- See the MOST Media Policy Statement: www.MOSTonline.org/Media_and_Multiples.pdf

- MOST also offers an article titled "Multiples in the Public Domain": www.MOSTonline.org/sunshop/index.php?l=product_detail&p=423

Chapter 10: An Ending and a New Beginning

T his portion of your journey to parenthood ends with the delivery of your babies, but a new section has just begun. This part will be filled with love, laughter, tears, joy and many diaper changes of course! We hope that this book has helped you with the pregnancy journey, and you have learned about your special pregnancy and babies. Obtaining the best care while pregnant and being proactive can help you have the healthiest babies possible. Listening to your body, asking questions and being prepared to deal with any complications also helps. Speaking with other parents of higher-order multiples in a secure setting, such as the MOST family forums, is invaluable! There you will learn from the experts: other parents who know EXACTLY what life is like with higher-order multiples.

No matter what your family goes through from this point forward, MOST is here to support you. Starting from the first year, NICU stay, coming home, sleep deprivation, early intervention, and through all the years thereafter: pre-school, elementary school, high school and beyond, MOST is with you every step of the way.

Helpful MOST Resources

In addition to all the resources provided through this book, we are also including links to some of the most popular and useful MOST resources available on our website. Additional resources are also available by calling the office at 631-859-1110, so please feel free to contact us. We are here to help.

- MOST's 500+ page website: www.MOSTonline.org/

- The MOST Supertwins 101: FAQs frequently asked questions about multiple births: www.MOSTonline.org/faqbf.htm

- The MOST by the Stages Expecting Multiples page: www.MOSTonline.org/stagespreg.htm

- Birth Weight Calculator and Convertor: www.MOSTonline.org/BirthWeightConvCombo.htm

- PreemieCare, a division of MOST: www.PreemieCare.org/

- The MOST by the Stages Infant Multiples page:
  http://www.mostonline.org/stagesnew.htm

- The MOST Infant Multiples Packet:
  www.MOSTonline.org/sunshop/index.php?l=product_detail&p=74 or
  Infant Multiples and Breastfeeding Combo Packet:
  www.MOSTonline.org/sunshop/index.php?l=product_detail&p=300

- MOST parenting packets, booklet and article bundles on topics like infant
  multiples, breastfeeding, toddler multiples and many more:
  www.MOSTonline.org/packages.htm

- Research on multiple births: www.MOSTonline.org/research.htm

- Statistics on higher-order multiples: www.MOSTonline.org/facts.htm

- Trained local support volunteers (MOST ACs) across the US and other
  countries: www.MOSTonline.org/volunteers.htm

- The MOST Family Support Forums: www.MOSTonline.org/forums.htm

- Bereavement support for families who experience a loss:
  www.MOSTonline.org/memorialview.html

- A listing of companies offering programs for free items, discounts and
  coupons for multiple-birth families: www.MOSTonline.org/freestuff.htm

- The MOST blog containing the latest media stories and medical news
  related to multiple births: http://www.mostonline.org/research.htm

- MOST's FREE monthly email newsletter (eNews):
  www.MOSTonline.org/MOSTNews.html

- Resources on multiples for professionals (doctors, educators, media professionals, etc.): www.MOSTonline.org/professionals.html

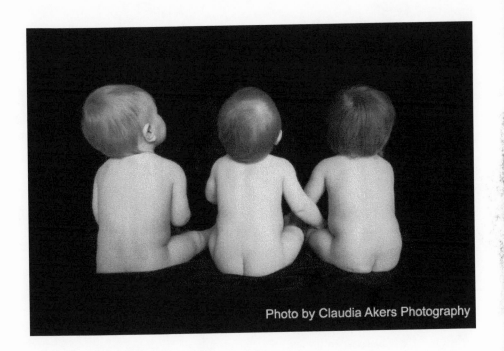

Photo by Claudia Akers Photography

The End

INDEX

A

abdominal binder, 165
abdominal ultrasound, 122, 123
abruptio placenta, 108
acetaminophen, 164
American College of Obstetricians
    and Gynecologists (ACOG), 33, 44,
    65, 136
amniocentesis, 124
amnion, 100
amnio-reduction, 101
amniotic sac, 29
anemia, **97**, 116
antinausea medications, 70
ART. *See* assisted reproductive
    technology
artificial insemination, 25
assisted reproductive technology, 22,
    24, 25

B

baby showers, 172
backache, 131
bacterial vaginosis (BV), 96
bed sores, 167
bedrest, 62, 78, 105, 106, 108, 126,
    135, **142**, 146, 148, 149, 155, 158,
    160, 168, 172, 173, 186, 197, 202
bedrest activity checklist, 142
Biophysical Profile. *See* BPP
bleeding. *See* vaginal bleeding
bleeding gums, **61**
blood pregnancy test level (hCG
    level), 23
BPP, 120, 121, 123
breast pumps, 160
breastfeed, 159
breastfeeding, 187

C

calorie intake, 82

carpal tunnel syndrome, 98, 117
Center for Loss in Multiple Birth
    (CLIMB), 112
Centers for Disease Control, 22, 36
cerclage, 72, 96, **126**, 127, 194
cerebral palsy, 74
cervical cerclage. *See* cerclage
cervical dilation, 108
cervical length, 72
Cesarean section. *See* C-section
chorion, 100
Chorionic villus sampling. *See* CVS
CL ultrasound, 72
combined deliveries, 191
comprehensive sonogram, 28
constipation, 80, 81
corticosteroids, 126
cramps, **131**
C-section, 61, 164, 190, 191, 192,
    193, 199
CVS, 71, 124, 125

D

delayed interval delivery (DID), 114,
    194
diamniotic-dichorionic, 100
diamniotic-monochorionic, 100
dilation and curettage, 113
dizygotic, 29
Doppler flow ultrasound, 123
Doppler velocimetry, 123
Down Syndrome, 70

E

early partial loss, **113**
effacement, 130
Elliott, Dr John, 32, 34, 56, 68, 76,
    140
Emergency Department (ED), 151
employment, 133, 143
epidural, 191, 193, 195

F

fertility medications, 22
Fetal Fibronectin (fFN), 135
fetal growth restriction, 106
fetal movement monitoring, 149
fetal reduction. *See* multifetal
    pregnancy reduction
Fifth Disease, 96
fraternal, 29
full-term, 26, 131, 134, 198

G

General Obstetrician, 41
gestational diabetes, **102**, 103
GIFT procedures, 69
gingivitis, 60
Group B strep (GBS), 96

H

hCG level, 23
HELLP syndrome, 105
Hemolysis, 105
High-Risk Specialist, 41
Home Uterine Activity Monitoring
    (HUAM), 136
household, 58, 145, 146, 171, 206
housework. *See* household
HUAM, 136, 137
hyperemesis, 69, 92, 93, 94, 116
hypertension, 104, 117
Hypertension. *See* preeclampsia

I

identical multiples, 29
indigestion, 82
Indocin. *See* Indomethacin, *See*
    Indomethacin
Indomethacin, 74, **138**
intestinal cramps, 131
intrauterine, 25
intrauterine fetal death (IUFD), 114
intraventricular hemorrhage (IVH), 63
IUGR. *See* fetal growth restriction

IUI, 25

K

Klein MD, Victor, 33

L

La Leche League, 160
Lactation Consultant, 160
Lamaze, 190
Laser therapy, 101
late partial loss, 114
late preterm, 198
layette, **176**
Level II ultrasound, 30, 121, 122
Level III NICU, 43, 46, 49, 50, 56,
    198
locchia, 196

M

mag. *See* magnesium sulfate
magnesium sulfate, 73, 74, **139**, 196
Maternal-Fetal Medicine Specialist. ,
    See MFMS
MFMS, 35, 41, 42, 47, 49, 57
miscarriage, 32, 71, 110
monoamniotic, 29, 30, 100, 101
monochorionic, 29, 72, 114
monozygotic, 29
morning sickness, 69, 79, 80, 92
MOST, **15**
MOST Medical Birth survey, 25, 30,
    62
Mothers of Supertwins, **15**
multifetal pregnancy reduction, **31**,
    34, 37
multiple births, **21**
multi-seat stroller, 176

N

naming babies, **159**
nausea, 80
necrotizing enterocolitis (NEC), 64

Neonatal Intensive Care Unit (NICU), **49**, **62**
Neonatologist, 51
NICU Notebook, 59, 64
nipple stimulation, 161
nitrazine paper, 109
Now I Lay Me Down to Sleep, 112
NT (nuchal thickness), 70
nursing sleep bra, 163
nutrition, 78
nutritional supplements, 84

O

oligohydramnios, 100
optimal weight gain, 79, 80
ovarian hyperstimulation, 69
ovulatory stimulating medications, 25

P

pediatrician, 56, 148, 156, 159
pelvic examinations, 73
pentazygotic, 29
Pergonal, 68
perinatal loss, 27
perinatologists, 27, 35, 56, 68, 74, 107, 126
periventricular leukomalacia (PVL), 63
pessary, 127
placenta previa, 108
Placental Abruption, 108
polyhydramnios, 100
poor fetal growth, 106
postpartum depression. *See* PPD
postpartum recovery, 195
PPD, 60, 198, 202, 207, 209, 211
PPROM, 32, 96, **109**, 110
preeclampsia, 60, 75, 86, **104**, 117
pregnancy tumors, 61
Pregnancy-Induced Hypertension, 104
premature, 33, 54, 60, 62, 65, 66, 69, 135, 197, 198, 199, 210
premature labor, 94, 96
preterm babies, 26, 27, 198, 202

preterm labor, 28, 46, 72, 73, 74, 85, 95, 98, 100, 110, 124, 127, **129**, 130, 131, 132, 133, 134, 135, 136, 151, 161, 194
Preterm Premature Rupture of Membranes. *See* PPROM
proactive pregnancy, 40
Procardia, **139**
progesterone, 75
Pruitic Urticarial Papules and Plaques of Pregnancy, 107
pubic bone separation, 164
pubic symphysis diastasis, 164
PUPPP, 106, 107

R

reacher, 168
reduction. *See* multifetal pregnancy reduction
Respiratory Distress Syndrome (RDS), 51
retinopathy of prematurity (ROP), 64
round ligament stretching, 99

S

sciatic nerve, 164
selective reduction. *See* multifetal pregnancy reduction
self-palpation, **134**
septostomy, 101
sibling, 29, 30, 53, **169**
single-embryo transfers, 25
skin changes, 103
Society for Assisted Reproductive Technology, 25
spontaneous conceptions, 25
spontaneous reabsorption, 113
steroids, 70, 73, 110, 126, 135
stillbirth, **110-111**, 114, 116, 118
stretch marks, 103, 165
stroller, 176
subchorionic hematoma, 108
Sudden Infant Death Syndrome (SIDS), 185

T

Tay-Sachs, 125
terbutaline, **137**
tetrazygotic, 29
tocolytic drugs, 73, 74
tocolytics, **137**
toradol, **139**
toxemia. *See* preeclampsia
transvaginal ultrasound, 23, **122**
trizygotic, 29
Twin-to-Twin Transfusion Syndrome
   (TTTS), 30, 72, 99, 117

U

ultrasound, **120**, 122
urinary tract infection, 86, **94**
uterine contractions, 131
UTI. *See* urinary tract infection

V

vaginal bacterial infections, 95
vaginal bleeding, 104, 105, **107**, 127,
   145, 190, 196
vaginal delivery, 190
vanishing twin, 113
vertex position, 191

W

waterproof pads, 179
weight gain, 78
WIC, 78

Y

yeast infections, 94

Z

zygosity, 29, 100

Made in the USA
San Bernardino, CA
15 June 2014